One Size CAN'T Fit All!

Integral Religion in a Fragmented World

Vicki Toale, OP

SophiaOmni Press

ISBN: 978-1516802203

Visit the companion website to this text at...
www.vickitoale.org

SophiaOmni Publishing
www.sophiaomni.org

DEDICATION

To the human imagination
that breaks through the inertia of culture and
allows our spirits to bloom and grow

BECAUSE THEY SAID SO

All that I have read, heard, and experienced lives and grows, consciously as well as unconsciously, in my imagination.

My ideas are a blend of all that has gone before and I am grateful to all [published or not] who have shaped my ideas and brought me where I am today.

Especially:
Ayn Rand for her vivid portrayal of life as a self-directed adult. She showed in a rarified form the importance of inner direction. Would that she took it a step further.

Science fiction and fantasy authors create worlds that stretch our horizons, keep the mystery alive and call forth new ways of being alive. In these fictional worlds our biases are irrelevant. We are challenged to face issues on their own merit. Thank you, J.R.R. Tolkein, C.S. Lewis, Marion Zimmer Bradley, Orson Scott Card, James Redfield, Daniel Quinn, Stephen Donaldson, Frank Herbert, J.K. Rowling, Starhawk.

Theologians: Walter Bruggemann, Matthew Fox, Diarmuid O'Murchu, Cynthia Bourgeault, Bishop John Shelby Spong, who search for new ways to express Mystery.

When I discovered Spiral Dynamics and Integral Theory, my world exploded, much of what I thought and taught fell into place, so many questions were contextualized. Thank you, Clare Graves, Don Beck, Ken Wilber, Steve McIntosh.

It turns out that we're all right. Yet, we are subject to an order that is just now being articulated. We ignore this at our own peril.

I am grateful for all who have shared my journey, especially those who have had to put up with my sometimes over-enthusiastic pursuit of Integral Theory as it reconfigures my understanding of religion.

TABLE OF CONTENTS

INVALUABLE INSIGHTS

TRUTH IN ADVERTISING

More advertisers are nuancing their product offerings these days. In many cases one size fits "most" has replaced one size fits "all." This is getting closer but in "most" cases the further you are from a size 16 to18 the "fit' becomes debatable. The basic premise of this book is that there is no way in our day and age, especially in Western society that one way of perceiving religion can possibly satisfy all believers. In fact, we are becoming more diverse.

When I heard Don Beck say that if you see things differently you act differently, my first reaction was: Duh! My second reaction was WOW! Most people agree that different mindsets result in a whole array of different preferences. Advertisers, movie and TV producers, clothes manufacturers, politicians, pretty much anybody who is seeking public attention knows this, and acts accordingly.

So how come religious leaders don't pay attention to this? If we pay attention to Integral Theory there are seven different ways to be Catholic, or Jewish, or Muslim, or Buddhist. Even many of those conscious of this, still serve the house special and expect all to relate to the religion *du jour*. Granted it is incredibly difficult to meet the needs of all.  Department stores have subdivided their clothing sections to appeal to different tastes and sizes without discriminating against one or the other. Can religion do the same?

As I learned more about Spiral Dynamics and Integral Theory I changed most of my teaching methods and began to teach a course called: What is religion? Over the years I have been pulling resources from various places often leaving students bewildered as they tried to see how the pieces fit together. Many students reacted so positively to the concepts that I knew I was on the right track. I finally decided to write it down as it makes sense to me and see where it leads.

In Part One I offer a brief introduction to the theory of Spiral Dynamics, as conceived by Clare Graves, and very brief synopses of the different growth theories. Further elaboration of human and the Divine relationships appear in Part Two. Part Three discusses both Spiral Dynamics and Ken Wilber's Integral Theory so that they can be applied to how the lower consciousness levels perceive religion in Part Four. I separated out the two higher levels as they have not yet been structurally experienced yet the seventh, the Integral Level, holds the key to ending the culture wars so many religions are embroiled in today. If we do make the "Leap" Clare Graves predicted, the eighth level, the Wholeview level will emerge allowing us to experience the connections without prejudicing the expressions.

I surrounded many of the chapters with quotes from science fiction and different insights from various authors to smooth the journey through our own and society's evolution thorough time. At the end of each part and at the end of the book I name and in that way credit those who are blazing the trail in so many ways.

PROLOGUE: FANTASTIK

On May 3, 2015, on the 55th anniversary of its opening "The Fantastiks" ["the world's longest running musical"] was scheduled to close. It was "saved" by two anonymous rich donors; but that's another story. What was so brilliantly begun in the "moonlight" of the 60s could no longer fill a two hundred seat theater. What happened?

This 1900 farce, recreated as a 1960 metaphor enchanted modern America. It spun a romantic tale that captured the imagination of those setting out to make their way, follow their dream. Idealism faced off with reality and they called it a draw.

A girl, who fears being normal, and a boy, who at twenty knows they way things really work, are madly in love. He begins by declaring that she is love, his mystery of love, claiming that she is better far than a metaphor could ever be! She is dazzled! She swoons! She accepts her role as his everything. A simple plot, a bit of manipulation and the first act closes in the moonlight with the star-crossed lovers about to "live happily ever after."

We no longer need El Gallo [the narrator] to tell us, as he told the audience, that all is not as it seems. The baby boomers, who were entering high school when it opened, have lived well into their second act with varying degrees of success. Our world seems as arthritic as their knees and hips. Nobody is flexible and everyone knows who's right and more especially who's wrong! In the "glaring sunlight" of our post postmodern world the stability that we were asked to try to remember seems unreal.

The metaphor is as tarnished as their cardboard moon. The postmodern, skeptical, ironic world rejects both idealism and realism. It has succeeded in our real world in relativizing both church and state. Today, love is more commodity than mystery. There seems to be no order or accepted value system. Bob Dylan who came to New York after dropping out of college in 1960 was David Letterman's, who hosted the Tonight Show from 1982 until 2015, last musical guest. Mr. Ironic, as Newsday called Letterman, went out to the tune "The Night They Called It a Day." Late night TV is now solely in the hands of the next generation.

Digital natives, those born after 1980, have grown up in a world of conflicting value systems. "Culture wars" have shaped the world of today's college student, as "The Fantastiks" shaped their grandparents'. What was it that their grandparents saw? What was so scenic that has turned so cynic today? In 1960 American society was at the top of its game. There was a sense of unity. We were beginning to address some of our inequalities. The future looked bright. Yet within eight years it all started to fall apart.

Culture rests on meaning. The role of religion in society is to articulate our meaning system. Religion is no longer an integral part of culture in most of the Western world. Yet it is passionately embraced by many in that world and most of the people in the Middle East and Southern Hemisphere. We speak of God and the world chooses up sides as if for a battle.

From the dawn of human consciousness, we have envisioned a spiritual world within or beyond our earthy one. For thousands of years we believed that our fate was determined by "God." Though beyond our comprehension, these mysterious powers, this Omnipotent Person, could be influenced by our behavior. God, defined in the Christian Scriptures as Love, is the generic term used by most humans when they think or speak of mystery: Ultimate Mystery, the Ground of All Being, the All-Powerful. We use metaphors because we are envisioning that which, we admit, cannot be defined.

Religion is a system of metaphors, beliefs, and behaviors, which has responded to Ultimate Mystery as perceived by specific people at specific times. It creates, and is created by culture. In a very generalized way, until and where modern consciousness became widely accepted, religion was the driving force of culture.   To remain vibrant religion must evolve as society does and in recent times it has failed to do so. The best way to understand why this has happened, is to look to Integral Theory.

Spiral Dynamics, a motivational theory, reveals the codes that shape human nature. Since society reflects the consciousness of its mature members, Clare Graves studied the kind of person people understand to be psychologically mature human beings. The realization that there are currently eight different, discrete levels of human consciousness which have been or still are considered to be mature by their adherents has revolutionized our understanding of humans and the societies they create. Each level sees the basic meaning of life in a radically different way. No wonder there is little social cohesion today.

Don Beck, his protégé, has developed and expanded Spiral Dynamics, showing that society develops as individuals do and all areas of life [including religion] are affected by and operate from significantly different levels of consciousness. The first six worldviews see others as a threat and soundly denounce their adherents. Only the two highest level can see the best insights of all as essential.

Therefore, there are eight different ways to be Catholic, or Jewish or Muslim, and as many to be atheist or agnostic. But which one is the right one? What would happen if they are all right? One size [level of consciousness] CAN'T fit all.

Isn't that fantastic?

Part I

ATTWII
[And That's The Way It Is]

The Paradigm

1

In the Beginning was the Question

The task of searchers is to set aside the egotism of perceptions and see as much of God as each can. We must literally set aside the smallness of our perceptions, the limits of our perceptions, and see what was hidden before.

Nancy Kress, Beggars Ride

Clare Graves was a professor of Psychology at Union College in Schenectady, New York from 1948–1978. He loved his work but was becoming more and more frustrated because, after studying all the psychological theories, students would approach him at the end of each semester and ask: **OK, professor, now that we learned them all, which one is right?** He was doubly frustrated because he had no answer to their question.

Clare Graves , a specialist in the theory of personality and its applications to industrial and medical problems, outlined his research in a 1971 talk at Washington School of Psychiatry. He had begun a major study to determine what people perceived as characteristic of the healthy adult person. Collecting pertinent data from his students and others over a long period of years, and after many tests and surveys, and much discussion, he developed his theory: The Emergent Cyclical Levels of Existence Theory. His interest focused on how human nature changes and he tracked that process by his students' responses. Rather than simply announce what is next, Graves' asked what is it that creates new systems, be they economic, political, religious, or educational? The attempt to find the deeper codes, the deeper meaning systems behind different worldviews, rather than surface level behaviors, eventually provided the tools needed to understand and therefore solve very serious problems that seemed diametrically opposed at the surface level.

Professor Graves found that human behavior can be broken down into eight patterns, or levels of existence. His theory suggests that every person falls somewhere between level one, a barely conscious human being, and level eight, a person conscious of his or her connection with all that exists. Society, made up of individuals functioning at these different levels can also be classified by these eight patterns. A pattern may not be evident in a culture until 10% of the population has manifested it. For example, when 10% of the North American colonists, the founding fathers and mothers of the United States, accepted the modern worldview, it enabled our democratic experiment to emerge. The rest of the country still operated from a premodern, hierarchical, royal, and traditional religious based worldview. [We will see the differences, when we look at how the balance shifts upward in the 1960s.]

What Graves discovered was that the different psychological theories he identified and then presented in his classes were not contradictory but merely different stages of development. By including biology, sociology, and systems theory as well, he demonstrated WHY people think in different ways about everything that affects them. The interaction of external life conditions and the capacity of the human person to adapt to new situations creates this pattern of development, both in the individual and in the society, which forms and is formed by those individuals. Here was the answer he was seeking: human nature continues to evolve. It is an open system. Neither the individual's nor society's consciousness is fixed. A definitely continuous, though discrete, development of consciousness marks the human journey.

The development was not linear. It alternated between two perspectives, one adjustive to external sources and the other self-directive. The latter group attempted to make this world fit them by expressing themselves to get what they wanted. The former was willing to deny or sacrifice self, to fit themselves to the world. The specific goals at each level evolved as new problems were encountered but the pattern remained the same. The new problems were caused by the solutions that had solved the previous ones.

The alternation between strong ego response and communal consideration plus the growth in complexity of life conditions creates a spiral. Graves called it a double helix, social DNA map. Here is how the stages that emerged during his study were categorized. [I am including references to a sample year presented at the end of chapter three to concretize the theory.]

The mature adult is a person who will:

1. Deny/Sacrifice Self for reward later. Defers to higher authority.	One Nation under God	1954
2. Express Self as self desires in a calculating fashion and at the expense of others; but not so much that others turn on you.	Boomers Blossom	1960
3. Deny/Sacrifice Self to get acceptance now. Answers to peer authority only.	Protests	1968
4. Express Self as self desires but not at the expense of others.	Next great change	????

The perceptions of this last group actually arose during the project. Graves was excited as he realized he was actually experiencing the emergence of next worldview. His insights led to predictions describing this "Momentous Leap" of consciousness that humankind is about to make. This amazing growth in consciousness will enable us to find more solutions than the rest of the levels put together. Actually, it will put together the insights of the previous levels. It is not only the next level; it is a radically new **integrated** vision that can save us from the destruction our bitter and divided world portends.

Many, including Einstein, have said that one cannot solve problems at same level of consciousness that created the problem. Carl Jung believed that we don't solve our problems. We simply outgrow them. While, as in all adult development, we can choose to remain at any level; what is needed to solve the problems we face today is for a significant number of people to rise to this next integral level of existence. In the process, and especially in crisis, regression to an earlier worldview is always a possibility. But the healthy personality, functioning reasonably well, wants to continue to grow. There is an infinite spark in the human soul that calls us to greater and deeper meaning in our lives.

Graves says several conditions are necessary for the emergence of higher level neurological behavior; there are chemical changes in the brain that accompany the changes in consciousness. The most basic condition is cognitive capacity. Children may imitate adult behavior;

but they must reach a certain competency to understand and embrace the reasons underlying such behavior. This implies the recognition and resolution of earlier level problems, and enough incentive to be willing to leave the familiar for the frontier. The process is not easy and many do regress in the face of the dissonance experienced.

Individuals change more easily than society. Early pioneers who achieve insights into the next possible worldview are often rejected as heretics or troublemakers. These obstacles must be overcome or ignored, if the insight is to begin to sustain what is always a great psychological jump. When ten percent of the population actually begins to practice this new way of behaving, the next level will begin to be manifested in society.

So, Who is Right?

If human values are not fixed and our consciousness expands if we remain psychologically and spiritually healthy, right becomes a matter of appropriateness not an absolute value.

Graves' Answer:

"What I am proposing is that the psychology of the mature human being is an unfolding, emergent, oscillating, spiraling process marked by progressive subordination of older, lower-order behavior systems to newer, higher-order systems as man's existential problems change. These systems alternate between focus upon the external world [Life Conditions] and attempts to change it; and upon the inner world [Mind Capacities] and attempts to come to peace with it."

"Graves' new psychological theory holds that human beings exist at eight different 'levels of existence.' At any given level, an individual exhibits the behavior and values characteristic of people at that level; a person who is centralized at a lower level cannot even understand people who are at a higher level. . . . Clare Graves outlines his new psychological theory, Spiral Dynamics, and what it suggests regarding humanity's future. Through history, says Graves, most people have

been confined to the lower levels of existence where they were motivated by needs shared with other animals. Now, Western society appears ready to move up to a higher level of existence, a distinctly human level. When this happens there will likely be a dramatic transformation of human institutions."

Claire Graves. *Human Nature Prepares for a Momentous Leap* [http://www.clarewgraves.com/articles_content/1974_Futurist/1974_Futurist.html]

Where do you live? Are you thinking of moving? [What kind of worldview makes you comfortable? Or uncomfortable?]

1. The first level is barely conscious and is often omitted in discussions.

2. **Magical** The world is full of mysterious powers.

   we obey desires of mystical spirit beings / show allegiance to clan and elders

3. **Powerful** The world is a jungle, only the strong survive.

   I value ruthless power, daring deeds, impulsive action at any cost / seek to avoid shame

4. **Orderly** The world is controlled by a Higher Power.

   we sacrifice self to the One True Way now to find meaning and purpose in life and everlasting peace

5. **Rational** The world is full of opportunities to make things better and bring prosperity.

   I strive for autonomy / seek the "good life" / play to win

6. **Communal** The world is the shared habitat of all creation.

   we must liberate humans from greed and dogma / promote community / share

7. **Integrative** The world is a chaotic organism where change is the norm.

   I work with existential reality / focus on competencies / find natural design

8. **Holistic** The world is a web of elegantly balanced forces.

   we blend / harmonize / focus on the good of all / network / less is more

Can you identify which of the above basic worldviews speak to you? [There may be more than one.]

2

Who Do You Think You Are?

"...are you a person, with volition and maybe some stubbornness and at least the capacity if not the actual determination to do something surprising, or are you a tool? A tool just serves its user. It's only as good as the skill of its user, and it's not good for anything else. So if you want to accomplish something special, something more than you can do for yourself, you can't use a tool. You have to use a person and hope the surprises will work in your favor. You have to use something that's free to not be what you had in mind."

Stephen Donaldson. The One Tree

Has anyone ever asked you that question? **Who do you think you are?** Usually the tone used carries a sense of disapproval and most of the time implies the person speaking doesn't like something about what you're doing! The "who we think we are" has offended their understanding of how we should be thinking or acting. And so the biting question is really meant not to be answered but to put us in our place. There are a whole series of questions that fall into the same category: What do you think you are doing? Where do you belong? Where do you think you are going? What makes you think you can do that? What do you mean by that?

So simple, and very annoying answers like, "I am the image of God" as the first chapter of the Bible tells us, or any claim to "inalienable" rights, would serve to aggravate the situation. Perhaps there is no answer to a question that is so obviously rhetorical. No answer is really expected. It is meant to diminish and demean.

While these questions are often used as a put-down, they are the most profound questions we face as humans. Thoughtful answers to these questions describe our essence. These are the questions, and answers, that expose our deepest longings, our hidden fears, and our basic stance toward life. In essence they are the basic religious questions.

We do have answers to these questions, whether we are aware of them or not, and they shape our lives. Our sense of who we are and what we're worth was formed when we were very young. It should evolve as we grow; but often are unconscious or even repressed. Our psyche remains fixed at this immature level and we never search for or articulate a mature sense of self that should grow as we do.

Charles Darwin is well on his way to being recognized as one of the greatest thinkers of the twentieth century. His insights, the conclusions he was bold enough to articulate as a result of long hours of thought and massive collaboration with other scientists, have changed human perception forever. In his *The Origin of Species*, Darwin meticulously laid out his theory, Natural Selection. Using pigeons, finches, and many of the species he encountered on his five-year journey around the world, he recognized that species change to gain advantage in their struggle for survival.

He charted it all on what he called the Tree of Life. This tree was very different from Genesis' tree in the Garden of Eden with branches beginning and ending and many different species developing from a common ancestor. He knew his research would cause great controversy, so he put off publishing his findings as long as he could. When Charles Darwin finally released his findings, evolution became the rage, and the outrage of the late 19th century. It explained so much; but it challenged even more.

Like Darwin, Clare Graves' research indicated that things are not fixed even within a human being. We do not stay the same. We evolve as we grow mentally, emotionally, spiritually. We develop. We know this. We experience this. And yet most often we pay little or no attention to the differences that have developed as we have reacted to life's circumstances over the centuries.

Human Development

Since the Enlightenment, the shift from a classical world consciousness, which began with the Infinite and worked "down," to an historical world view, to one which begins with the human person and then looks toward God, has been steadily gaining in popularity. To start with the human person and to attempt to examine that person's beliefs and behaviors however he or she reacts to different stimuli, opens the way for deeper insight into the human growth process. The advantage gained in such study enables us to deal with greater and greater complexity in life conditions.

Many psychologists, inspired by Darwin's concept of biological evolution, began to look more closely at human cognitive and psychological growth. It's obvious that children and adults do not think alike. Can the maturation process be predicted? Are there patterns or stages of growth that can be identified? How does one move through the different stages of growth? Research does confirm that as they grow, human shift how they perceive and interpret the world and how their values change as they begin to think in new ways.

What follows is a brief summary of some of the early pioneers in developmental psychology; some influenced Clare Graves and some benefitted from his research. I have chosen the ones that will give enough background to put Spiral Dynamics and Integral Theory into the larger context of human growth and development. If you are not familiar with, or would like to pursue the research further, primary resources and much less generalized information about the various theories are noted in Basic Resources at the end of Part One.

The Beginnings

James Mark Baldwin is considered one of the founders of developmental psychology. He was an American philosopher and psychologist who made important contributions to early psychology, psychiatry, and the theory of evolution. Baldwin's *Mental Development in the Child and the Race: Methods and Processes* (1894) and *Handbook of Psychology (Feeling and Will)* which appeared in 1891 made a vivid impression on Jean Piaget. It was Baldwin in the last decade of the 19th century and Clare Graves in the 1950s and 60s who were among the first to show possible ways the theory could be applied practically. Ken Wilber acknowledges influence of both of these men on his early work.

Early connection between religion and human growth:

Carl Gustav Jung (1875-1961) was a Swiss psychiatrist, an influential thinker and the founder of analytical [Jungian] psychology. Jung is considered as the first modern psychologist to state that the human psyche is "by nature religious" and to explore it in depth. Carl Jung held that that the general neurosis of our time stems from a lack of spiritual connection with the unconscious forces of our personality. It is only in conflict situations that these forces become conscious. Jung saw the value of the great religions calling us forward to new life as a means to a better, richer, healthier life than one that can only look back at what was.

Cognitive Development:

Jean Piaget was a Swiss cognitive theorist; he remains one of the most influential researchers in the nature and development of human intelligence. In the 1920s he studied how children think. Noticing that there was a gradual progression from intuitive to scientific to socially acceptable responses to the questions he asked; he explained in his cognitive development theory that children actively construct knowledge as they explore and manipulate the world around them. He believed that as children grow their brains develop and move through four distinct stages that are characterized by differences in thought processes.

Jean Piaget pioneered the research in cognitive development. He saw it as a dynamic system of continuous change. Knowing is not just seeing; it is experiencing, understanding, judging, and believing. Piaget's theory outlines the process of successive qualitative changes of cognitive structures, each structure and its concomitant change deriving logically and inevitably from the preceding one. These changes are hierarchical, each successive stage carrying forward in modified and augmented form the operations of the previous stage, and invariant, each stage building upon the previous one so that none can be skipped.

The four development stages as described by Piaget:

1. Sensorimotor stage: from birth to age two. The children experience the world through movement and their five senses. During the sensorimotor stage children are extremely egocentric, meaning they cannot perceive the world from others' viewpoints. During the sensorimotor period the infant adapts to the environment through the senses and by means of motor activities. Beginning with vague awareness and simple reflexes, patterns of behavior, are gradually refined into more distinct and accurate perceptions of the environment, accompanied by well-coordinated motor responses.

2. Preoperational stage: Piaget's second stage starts when the child begins to learn to speak at age two and lasts until the age of seven. Thinking and actions are no longer tied to real objects and events.

The preoperational child can manipulate objects and events symbolically, representing them by images and, words. The ability to treat objects as symbolic of other objects is an essential characteristic of this stage.

Preoperational thought is superficial, primitive, and generally confused. It remains egocentric, children in this period still are unable to take the role or point of view of others. In solving problems, the preoperational child primarily focuses on, and responds to, the aspects of the immediate environment that are perceived directly. The child will concentrate on a single feature of a problem and fail to take into account other equally important dimensions.

3. Concrete operational stage: from ages seven to eleven. At seven the child, now in the period of concrete operations is able to focus on several dimensions of a problem at the same time and to understand the relationships among, these dimensions. Related to this recognition is the understanding of reversibility, the idea that, in thinking steps can be retraced, actions can be cancelled and an original situation can be restored. This realization renders the child's, thought much more flexible and less egocentric. He or she becomes capable of logical processes or what Piaget calls operations. In mental operations, actions performed on objects are carried out internally. The achievements of the operational period reflect the child's increased ability to understand relationships among objects and events.

4. Formal operational stage: from age eleven to sixteen and onwards a person becomes capable abstract reasoning. Abstract thought is the hallmark of the most advanced stage of intellectual development, the stage of formal operations. Children in the formal operational stage display more skills oriented towards problem solving, often in multiple steps. Thinking in terms of logical propositions and applying logical rules and reasoning to abstract problems are the essences of mature intellectual ability.

It is important to note at this point that while adolescents (and adults) are capable of thinking in this abstract, logical way, they do not necessarily do so. For cultural, educational, and intellectual, reasons, many do not develop formal operational thinking or flexible problem solving skills.

Piaget's stages are important to understand. The different levels or stages that Clare Graves identified can only be achieved if one has the cognitive capacity to think at that level. Yet just because one has developed the necessary skills does not mean that he or she will automatically see the world in a more complex manner. The skills are necessary but not sufficient for a change of worldview. Other conditions must also be in place.

Human needs and motivation:
Abraham Maslow was an American psychologist, and a contemporary of Clare Graves, Maslow is best known for creating a hierarchy of needs theory. His work focused on people fulfilling innate human needs in priority, which if satisfied culminates in self-actualization. In Jung's writings, this is the ultimate goal, toward which each individual is striving. While many theories exist to explain this process, Maslow's is one of the most respected. Human motives, he realized, can be broadly categorized as growth motives or deprivation motives. They are arranged in a developmental hierarchy; where the lowest deficiency or deprivation needs must be met before a person can pur-

sue needs higher in the hierarchy.

The most basic deprivation needs of the human person are for water, food, and sleep (physiological needs). These are followed by safety needs, characterized by the avoidance of pain and discomfort. When these needs are satisfied, the needs for belongingness (for love and intimacy) become significant; and these, in turn, are superseded by needs for esteem (approval of others and of self). Maslow later expanded these levels but retained the basic delineation of deficiency and being which parallel Graves' First and Second Tier value systems.

It is only when all of the deficiency needs have been met that actualization tendencies or growth motives can be expressed strongly. The achievement of a healthy self-esteem enables a person to face others, including God, with self-confidence and a readiness to blend his or her life with theirs. Growth motives can be expressed as Being-characteristics or values paralleling the characteristics of fully mature human people: truth, goodness, beauty, wholeness, aliveness, completion, justice, order, simplicity, playfulness, and self-sufficiency. The problem with this is that Maslow himself admits that few make it to full actualization. Yet we expect, at least subconsciously, such behavior of all adults no matter what their level of development or circumstances of life.

As Jung acknowledged many adults settle for less than their potential, Maslow postulated a "Jonah Complex", the fear of one's own greatness or the running away from one's own best talents. We fear our best as well as our worst, though in different ways. Not only are we unsure about our own highest potential, we are also in conflict and ambivalence over the same possibilities in others.

Maslow's impression was that the greatest people simply by their presence and by being what they are, make us, feel aware of our lesser worth. Allied to this dynamic is the awe before excellence which makes us aware of the universality of the fear of direct confrontation with a god or the godlike. The experience of peak experiences, variously described by Maslow as moments of pure happiness, rapture or ecstasy, a sense of oneness with the world and a feeling of having perceived an ultimate truth, are fleeting leaving with us a fear of being torn apart, or of losing control until we reach the higher levels of consciousness where we judge less absolutely.

Faith Development:

James Fowler was an American theologian whose research in the area of faith development uncovered the patterns of faith transformation. He discovered that humans pass through recognizable stages as they grow in spiritual maturity. Influenced by Piaget's structural development theory, Fowler interviewed people of all ages and religious affiliations in Boston, Chicago and Toronto. By asking them to describe their spirituality, Fowler's was able to identify his six Stages of Faith Maturity, which again corresponds beautifully to the levels of Spiral Dynamics and Integral Theory. The Integral Institute paid formal homage to Fowler's work in 2007 when they awarded him the first Integral Spirituality Award for lifetime achievement.

Faith is about structuring meaning as a result of cognitive and emotional development. This structuring comes about as we interact with society. Fowler does not see faith as a noun, a system of beliefs to be accepted as true or rejected as false; but as a verb, an act of commitment. Faith is a way of being in relationship with another. Because of our limited experiences we have no choice but to have "faith" in our fellow humans as well as the divine. Faith is accompanied by belief, commitment, love and risk-taking.

Just a note; here we are talking about **how** we believe, not **what** we believe. People at the same level process their perceived truths in the same way, but can adhere to very different belief systems. Developmental changes refocus the way we interact with whatever it is we accept as true. People at different levels perceive the same data in different ways, because of their capacity to analyze and synthesize experiences more or less broadly.

I will briefly outline the stages Fowler identified but discuss the implications of these levels in Part Four when we look at each stage and the approach to religion it generates.

The Stages

Fowler recognized a pre-stage of **Undifferentiated Faith** during which the seeds of trust, courage, hope and love are fused in an undifferentiated way. The emergent strength of faith at this stage is the foundation of basic trust and the relational experience of mutuality with the one providing primary love and care. It can be compared with Graves' first instinctual level.

1. The first stage is called **Intuitive-Projective Faith.** By two our perceptions are colored by the examples, moods, and actions of the invisible faith of our parents. I will call it the **Wonder-full Stage.** Magic happens all the time at this level of belief. The child continues to encounter new things for which he or she has as yet no fixed context so surprise and fantasy flourish. Walt Disney has mastered the skill of engaging the child, and the child in all of us, at this stage. It is easy to wish upon a star when so many wonderful things happen regularly. The gift or emergent strength of this stage is the birth of the imagination, the ability to unify and grasp the world in powerful images that do create a magical kingdom.

2. The second stage, **Mythic-Literal Faith**, begins at approximately age seven. Now introduced to our educational system and confronted by the larger world, the child is able to identify with the stories, beliefs and observances that represent belonging to his or her community. John Walsh dubbed this the **In-doctrination Stage** because  we are confronted with the doctrines, the beliefs, and the correct behaviors of our "tribe." At this level of cognitive ability we accept the story literally. Symbolic language is still one dimensional and meaning is assumed to be literal fact. At this stage the meaning is both carried by and trapped in the narrative.

3. Fowler calls the third stage **Synthetic-Conventional**. As a person's world expands, faith must provide a coherent orientation in the midst a more complex and diverse range of involvements. While beliefs and values are deeply felt, they have not been reflected on explicitly or systematically. It is a conformist stage in the sense that belief and behavior are tied to the expectations of significant others. This is the **Parade Stage** and that word accurately describes its focus. Stage three typically has its rise and ascendancy in adolescence, but for many adults it becomes their permanent place of equilibrium. From this stage while cognitive capacity enables growth, it is not sufficient to produce it. Circumstances and the weight of traditional values can easily prevent further emancipation.

** ** The transition from stage three to four involves clashes with authority and experiences which undermine one's previously unchallenged understanding of the world. We may choose to leave the parade and chart our own course. This will become critical as we look at

the crisis of becoming an adult and religious experience. This does not imply that people who remain at stage three are unhappy. Yet as the world becomes more complex, many who remain at this level of faith-consciousness find it difficult to deal with what they see as betrayal and chaos.

4. The movement to **Individuative-Reflective** faith is significant. Now the person is challenged to take seriously the burden and responsibility for his or her own commitments, lifestyle, beliefs and attitudes. This is primarily a stage of struggle as the fledgling adult must claim self-direction by means of critical evaluation of all that has gone before as well as whatever may lie ahead. The self now claims an identity no longer defined by the expectations of others. It expresses its own intuitions in terms of an explicit system of meaning. The person typically translates symbols into conceptual meanings. This is a demythologizing stage, everything becomes subject to scrutiny. This stage can be called the **I've-got-to-be-me Stage**, whether this image is projected timidly or with great gusto. Stage four is concerned with boundaries. Where do I stop and you begin? How can I be authentically me? Who do I think I am?

5. The fifth stage is now called **Conjunctive** although the original name, **Paradoxical-Consolidative** was more descriptive. We realize the complexity of life and are willing to accept other points of view. In the **You-could-be-right-too Stage**, we move from logic to the paradoxical. We are able to see the deeper meaning of the symbols that enchanted us earlier. Meaning lies beyond the literal. Alive to new paradigms and able to see truth in apparent contradictions, this stage strives to unify or at least hold together opposites in mind and experience, and to achieve relative balance amid complexity and chaos.

6. According to Fowler, **Universalizing Faith** is exceedingly rare. The persons best described by it have generated faith commitments which include the environment and all beings. They identify deeply with humanity in general, and spend themselves in service of worldwide issues having made consciously or unconsciously a life commitment to justice and love. People at the **Compassionate Connection Stage** know that all life is interconnected. They are able to feel the pain and joy of all are often seen as a threat to the existing order. As more

people move into Graves' Integral consciousness more people will be able to reach this level than was previously possible.

7. Unfolding . . . Fowler has acknowledged that higher stages may emerge as human consciousness continues to expand. Piaget and Maslow also admitted this possibility. Clare Graves has named higher levels of human values; the Integral community continues to chart the evolution of human potential.

When it comes to religious faith there is the added dimension of "Ultimate Reality." We have all been influenced by our cultures. Some still march to foundational cultural tunes. Others are writing new music to dance in celebration of the reality of new relationships with the Deity.

The Bible begins: In the beginning God created the heavens and the earth. We can only know of the beginning in the true sense as we live now, and embrace it in the middle, between beginning and end. Being in the middle of anything is most disconcerting. There is within us a desire to know, to have fixed reference points, and definite boundaries. Where are we going? Where have we been? Who are we? Why are we? Questions such as these plague us as they did our spiritual ancestors. Yet at the same time we seek to unlock the mystery of life, to free ourselves from ambiguity and follow the less travelled path which leads to new life.

Consciousness Itself:

Jenny Wade, influenced by brain researchers, developmental psychologists and mystics alike, developed a continuum of psychospiritual development that stretches from before birth through all life's stages and includes after death experiences. She extrapolated her data from the leading theorists because she believed that consciousness is the ground of all thought. While her progression is both grounded in and congruent to conventional theories, she moves into an area resisted by conventional psychology but very much a part of mystical experience. By recognizing the cosmos as a seamless whole where matter and spirit are connected she searches for greater understanding of the whole person.

I mention her work here because, while it is not well known, it is an original and excellent synthesis of the different theories and she offers an interesting insight about the relationship between achievement and egalitarian consciousness, or the modern and postmodern way of perceiving reality. She holds them as alternative paths while Don Beck insists that one must follow the other. We will explore this in greater depth in Part Four.

One Size CAN'T Fit All!
So Why Do We Act Like It Does?

All Tied Up: If a baby elephant is tied to a stake by a rope when it is young, it becomes conditioned to the fact that the rope is stronger that it is. So, when a full grown elephant, which is now so physically strong that no rope can hold it, is tied to a stake, it never even tries to break free.

This exemplifies the basic premise of this book. While there is more and more evidence in all fields of study that evolution drives the universe, that change is constant, and growth inevitable; there is also more and more resistance, often vehement, to the application of these modern theories to our moral and spiritual lives. When we take these theories seriously, and live accordingly, we will be better able to communicate with one another and recognize the good that exists at each level of existence. We will realize that the goodness of one level need not be sacrificed as we mature to the next.

The alternative is to cling, consciously or unconsciously, to our current level of consciousness, with its pathologies as well as its gifts. In rejecting all other worldviews, either above or below our level, we end up limited to "our" eighth of reality, renouncing all those with different perceptions. This is where we are today; fighting culture wars that need not exist. Yet they "tie" us, as falsely as the elephant is tied, to what is or what was.

Integral theory knows the causes of the divisions we face today. They are not what we think they are! It offers a way to work more effectively with others. Surface differences do not cause such deep division. The underlying meaning systems we judge by bind us. To get where we all want to be, we must work against the assumptions of culture. We must reject the clichés so easily hurled at one another each day.

The same conditioning that can control a full grown elephant inhibits otherwise mature human beings from true insight; the power of perception can literally hold us prisoner. Our cultural assumptions, **our conscious and subconscious clinging to old worldviews can restrict our understanding of what is now possible.** As Hamlet said, "thinking makes it so!" The question remains. What does it mean to be a fully mature human person today?

Basic Resources for Part One

Cowan, Christopher and Natasha Todorovic, ed. *The Never Ending Quest: Clare Graves*

Explores Human Nature. Santa Barbara: ECLET Publishing, 2005.

Fowler, James, *Stages of Faith: The Psychology of Human Development and the Quest for Meaning*. San Francisco: Harpercollins College Div., 1981.

Fowler, James and Sam Keen. *Life Maps: Conversations on the Journey of Faith*. Texas: W Pub Group, 1978.

Graves, Clare. *Levels of Human Existence*. Transcription edited by William Lee. Santa Barbara: ECLET Publishing, 2002.

Jung, Carl and Joseph Campbell, ed. *The Portable Jung*. New York: Penguin Books, 1971.

Maslow, Abraham. *The Farther Reaches of Human Nature*. New York: Viking Press, 1971.

Piaget, Jean and Barbel Inhelder. *The Psychology of the Child*. New York: Basic Books, 1969.

Wade, Jenny. *Changes of Mind: A Holonomic Theory of the Evolution of Consciousness*. New

York: State University of New York Press, 1996.

Wilber, Ken. *Integral Psychology*. Boston: Shambhala Publications, 2000.

Part II

TMSAISTI
[That's My Story and
I'm Sticking to It]

The Human, The Divine, The
Relationship

3

What Does it Mean to Be Human?

You come of the Lord Adam and the Lady Eve, and that is both honor enough to erect the head of the poorest beggar, and shame enough to bow the shoulders of the greatest emperor of earth.

C.S. Lewis. Chronicals of Narnia

What does it mean to be a human being, independent of culture and its incredible influence on our lives? What are we capable of doing? What makes us special? Or are we special? These questions and history's varied answers fill libraries and provoke the heated debates that characterize our world today.

Spiral dynamics is a bio-psycho-social [and I would add spiritual] framework that helps our understanding of human relationships. The basic concept is that in all areas of human consciousness we become more capable of dealing with complexity if/as we mature. So, let's go back to our basic questions.

What Do You Think You Are?
Biology: Body / Brain

Humans are bipedal primates, belonging to the mammalian species. The first "humans" evolved in Africa approximately 200,000 years ago. What Charles Darwin saw and understood about evolution in the abstract, has been verified and enlarged upon by DNA research. Darwin's contribution to evolutionary theory, natural selection, showed how species descended from common ancestors.

Any change, however slight, in a plant or animal that created an advantage in a given situation ensured a better chance of survival and greater opportunity for repro-  duction. Over time those that possessed the advantageous characteristic would dominate the population and the change would become a permanent characteristic of the species. Just as breeders use artificial selection to improve or produce desired characteristics in dogs or flowers, nature selects and improves species thus enhancing their chance of survival.

Descent from a common ancestor does not mean the apes became human. Darwin used the concept of the Tree of Life to demonstrate the relationships among species. Branches are subdivided into lesser branches as different traits are acquired and strengthened by natural selection. Humans and apes descended from a common ancestor five to seven million years ago. We continue to adapt as do our animal brothers and sisters; yet evolution brought us into a new category.

The key biological features the earliest humans developed:

Upright Posture	which frees the hands for other tasks, makes childbirth harder, and is more prone to lower back pain.
Extraordinary Brains	facing challenges evolved larger and more complex brains which carried a greater ability to reason and necessitates a longer childhood,
Speech	the human larynx evolved 350,000 years ago which gave greater us capacity for articulation.
Hands	primates have opposable thumbs; but the human thumb is more flexible allowing a stronger grip and more dexterity.

Who Do You think You Are?
Psychology: Consciousness / Mind

We are a product of what Holmes Rolston III calls the Third Big Bang. In his book, *Three Big Bangs*, he meditates on each of the quantum jumps that have occurred during the universe's thirteen billion year existence. First, there was nothing, and then there was matter and energy. The second bang, produced life where there had been no life before. Finally there was mind: *Homo sapiens*, the ones who know. After each revolution, evolution continued. About 200,000 years ago, *Homo sapiens* became *homo sapiens sapiens*, the ones who know that they know. And here we are. What makes us different from the animals and the earlier life forms on the evolutionary spiral? What is it that is inherent in our species alone?

Because of our mind, our consciousness, we are aware of possibilities, humans are freed from instinctual behavior. We can:

Choose	in every situation we have the power to fashion our our response to different stimuli.
Use language and symbols	which allow for deeper levels of communication and stronger relationships and the ability to develop ways to cope in an unpredictable world.
Think abstractly	the ability to calculate, question, analyze, see the relationship between cause and effect which leads to better choices.
Be curious	we thrive on new information.
Remember	our memory enables previous experiences to teach us lessons.
Imagine	we see what can be, to change what is, we can dream
Accept paradox	we live with ambiguity, we can make connections.

Be creative	we invent and improve tools, to change our environment rather than be subject to it.
Achieve	we plan and create for the future.
Laugh	we react to absurdity or irony in situations and share that with others.
Hope	we believe in a better future.

Where Do You Belong?
Social Sciences: relationships / Emotions

Humans are social by nature. We need relationship. We have survived and actually thrived because we are capable of self-expression, exchanging ideas and social organization. Culture gives us a sense of belonging, develops and embodies our meaning systems, frames our daily lives and our expectations, and provides a sense of security. It is our inherent interdependence that makes us strong. We are able to meet challenges and create beneficial surroundings because of our organizational skills.

Each culture organizes itself according to its specific viewpoint, but all societies must deal with economic, political and cultural issues, if they are to survive. We are a product of our traditions as well as our decisions. Those in a society that differ too greatly from the rest often feel isolated and anxious and may suffer from low self-esteem.

The way values are interpreted may differ because of location or levels of consciousness; but the basic principles of human life remain the same. Humanity has been endowed with basic natural principles and values. We expect:

Honesty	frankness and candor
Fairness	justice
Kindness	consideration and compassion
Respect	recognition, deference and appreciation
Integrity	honor and reliability
Mutuality	empathy and support

Where Do You Think You're Going?
Theology / Religious Studies: The Human Spirit

One of the greatest contributions integral consciousness is making to the world is the reclamation of the spiritual. Since the time of the Enlightenment, many have viewed spirituality as an aspect of our mental faculty. Yet this capacity, great as it is, is finite. It is our spirit, our higher self, our animating principle that relates to the infinite. From the dawn of our consciousness, we have been aware of the presence of powers and spirits. Our spiritual capacity to imagine and to organize grew out of an inner sense that we are neither alone nor in charge.

We live in awe and fear of that which we don't understand. The numinous, the mystical, "God" both attracts and terrorizes. It is our spirit that enables us to face such delight and uncertainty. Developing our spirituality, the expression of our spirit in time and space, guides our mind and emotions in their search for meaning. Here is where we connect with the infinite ones. Here is the home of hope. Here we make the choice to be fully human. Our spirits are indeed restless without this connection.

Wonder and awe are basic human traits. There is no one more open to divine possibility than a three year old child. What happens to us if we do not cultivate this gift? We become obsessed with boundaries and borders and fail to see horizons. We focus on answers and dismiss mystery. We center on the here and now and miss the fact that our true destiny is beyond. Life as we know it now is but a step in an large evolutionary spiral, not the last stop on a finite journey.

Spirituality enables the deepest dimension of our lives to inform and remind our body, mind and emotions of our true destiny as human beings. It includes:

Wonder	surprise and astonishment at the wonder of creation
Faith	commitment to the higher powers
Patience	endurance and serenity in the face of our finitude
Gratitude	appreciation of all that we have been given
Determination	strength of mind and resolve to grow and change
Hope	optimism and anticipation of the good that is possible
Humility	acceptance of who we truly are as humans, our strengths and our weaknesses

The Best of Times, the Worst of Times

Just as there are stages in human development, our society, considered as a compilation of people living together in a more or less ordered community, has passed though discernible changes in worldviews. One broad division often used to explain the different stages is the **Premodern, Modern, and Postmodern World.** Using three pivotal moments in recent United States history, 1954, 1960, and 1968, let me set the mood for those who weren't with us yet, and remind those of us who were there of how much and how quickly we've changed.

The Premodern World: From the Beginning - Ends in the 17th Century

The world is in the hands of the gods who control nature's forces for their own interests. They cannot be forced to do things humans want; but they can be entreated. Power lies in a new religious type of thought, the ability to communicate with the gods. Ultimately in the West this power is concentrated in the Catholic Church. The Bible contains the covenant made with God which, if kept, will bring safety in this world and happiness in the next. In 1954, most of American life was still influenced by this worldview.

The American Dream and Religion: 1954

I chose this date, to epitomize the premodern world because it was the year that Congress added the words "One nation, under God" to the Pledge of Allegiance. ["In God We Trust" was adopted as the official motto of the United States in 1956.] Because of the results of the New Deal and the GI Bill, more and more people were able to realize their share of the American Dream. President Eisenhower had been in office for two years. Prayer was an integral part of government meetings and the school day.

On the international scene, Dwight D. Eisenhower pledged United States support to South Vietnam and gave his "domino theory" speech during a news conference. Senator Joseph McCarthy began hearings investigating the United States Army for being "soft" on Communism.

The main immigration port-of-entry at Ellis Island closed permanently. The first nuclear-powered submarine, the USS Nautilus, was launched.

At home, many African-American GIs were denied the privileges that so enriched the lives of their European-American comrades. We did take some tentative steps to deal with racial inequality. US Defense Department announced elimination of all racially segregated regiments in our Armed Forces. The Boy Scouts of America desegregated on the basis of race. The Supreme Court, in Brown v. Board of Education, ruled unanimously that segregated schools are unconstitutional.

President Eisenhower put forward his plan for an interstate highway system. The first mass vaccination of children against polio began in Pittsburgh. J. Hartwell Harrison and Joseph Murray performed the world's first successful kidney transplant in Boston. The IBM 650 magnetic drum calculator established itself as the first mass-produced computer, with the company selling 450 in one year.

Norman Rockwell appeared in a national print ad which read, "Light their life with faith. Bring them to worship this week." This advertisement was sponsored by Protestant, Catholic, and Jewish lay people in an effort to encourage weekly religious service attendance, it was aimed especially at parents and their children. 79% of adults acknowledged church membership, while 63% attended church weekly. [This number peaks in 1959; hence the choice of our second year, 1960.] The first Church of Scientology is established in Los Angeles, California.

Molloy College in Rockville Centre broke ground for Quealy Hall, its first building.

Plans to build Disneyland in California were announced. Bill Haley & His Comets recorded *Rock Around the Clock*, starting the rock and roll craze. Elvis Presley recorded his first two songs. The Miss America Pageant was broadcast on television for the first time. Marilyn Monroe married baseball player Joe DiMaggio. The first issue of Sports Illustrated magazine is published in the United States. The TV dinner was introduced by the American entrepreneur Gerry Thomas. "Father Knows Best" premiered. These were the "Happy Days" that the TV show depicted.

Where do you see examples of premodern thinking today?

The Modern World: Lasts from the 17th Century Until the 1920s

The world is a machine, a clock, that God wound up and left humans to run. Science and pure reason replaced religion as the focus of power. Its basic principles include: self-sufficiency, belief in inevitable progress, the assumption that knowledge is inherently good. Democracy and capitalism, replaced hierarchical authority structures. The human conscience is now seen as capable of creating its own set of values. Although the modern period had been intellectually accepted for a while, it was only in the sixties that it captured the American soul.

Only in America: 1960

The Baby Boomers, the huge cohort of babies born right after War World II, began high school. Elvis Presley received his honorable discharge from the U.S. Army and returned home from Germany, after

being away on military duty for two years. *The Fantasticks*, the world's longest-running musical, opened. It has played for fifty-five years to date. The newly named Beatles began a forty-eight night residency in Hamburg, West Germany. Bob Dylan dropped out of college and headed for New York.

It was the year of the following firsts: aluminum cans, Domino's Pizza, the Xerox machine, and the telephone answering machine. The pacemaker was invented. Joanne Woodward was awarded the first star on the Hollywood Walk of Fame. Rachel Carson finished the research for her book **Silent Spring,** the first warning about environmental destruction. Harper Lee published her first novel **To Kill a Mockingbird,** which later won the Pulitzer Prize for the best American novel of 1960. The world population reached 3,021,475,001.

Gas cost twenty-five cents a gallon. The countries of Iran, Iraq, Kuwait, Saudi Arabia, and Venezuela formed OPEC. Castro nationalized all US owned businesses, including refineries, factories and casinos, in Cuba. The Irish Republican Army started its fight against British domination in Ireland. The United States announced that 3,500 American soldiers would be sent to Vietnam. The Sharpeville massacre in South Africa resulted in more than 69 dead, 300 injured.

The United States began a period of dramatic social change. A new consciousness began to emerge.   Dwight D. Eisenhower signed the

Civil Rights Act of 1960 that established federal inspection of local voter registration polls and introduced penalties for anyone who obstructed anyone's attempt to register to vote. Senator John F. Kennedy was elected president.

In Greensboro, North Carolina, Joseph McNeil, Franklin McCain, Ezell Blair, Jr. and David Richmond began a sit-in at a segregated Woolworth's lunch counter. Although they were refused service, they were allowed to stay at the counter. The event triggered many similar non-violent protests throughout the Southern United States, and six months later the original four protesters were served lunch at the same counter.

> **Where do you see examples of modern thinking today?**

The Postmodern World: Lasts from the 1920s until the 1980s

Post-modern is the generic term used to express our general dissatisfaction with the failed promises of the modern world. Intellectual know-how had not delivered the good life for all. The lethal consequences of industrialism were becoming more and more apparent. Political promises were seen as empty rhetoric in the face of war and violence. The modern claim of unprecedented progress was not panning out. Religion became further alienated and actually dissociated from culture. The previously unassailable myth of salvation history had been discredited. Western encounters with leaders of other world religions had shaken the monopolistic claim of Judeo-Christian theology.

When Einstein's Theory of Relativity undermined Newton's scientific principles, modern certainty began to be replaced by the relativism that pervades today's culture. Postmodernism rejects both premodern religious dogma and modern scientific thought, claiming that there is no certain knowledge and all assumptions must be questioned. There is no outside authority that must be followed, and there is no such thing as objective observation.

Its seeds took root and began to bloom in the American psyche in 1968.

The Shape of the Next Generation: 1968

Rowan & Martin's Laugh-In debuted on NBC. NET televised the very first episode of *Mister Rogers' Neighborhood*. The Beatles announced the creation of Apple Records and released their self-titled album popularly known as the *White Album. 60 Minutes,* which is still on the air as of 2015, debuted on CBS.

The Standard & Poor's 500 index closed above 100 for the first time. The semiconductor company Intel is founded. In San Francisco, Douglas Engelbart publicly demonstrated his pioneering hypertext system, NLS, together with the computer mouse. U.S. spacecraft *Apollo 8* entered orbit around the Moon. Astronauts Frank Borman, Jim Lovell and William A. Anders became the first humans to see the far side of the Moon and planet Earth as a whole. The crew read a passage from the book of Genesis. Yale University announced it was going to admit women. Saddam Hussein became Vice Chairman of the Revolutionary Council in Iraq after a coup d'état.

Martin Luther King, Jr., was killed, sparking violent protests in more than 115 American cities. U.S. presidential candidate Robert F. Kennedy was shot and killed in Los Angeles. U.S. President Lyndon B. Johnson signed the Civil Rights Act of 1968. Popularly known as the Fair Housing Act, it prohibits discrimination concerning the sale, rental and financing of housing based on race, religion, national origin and sex.

Television, so influential in forming the identity of this generation, became the tool of choice for the revolutionaries. They fought their battles not just on streets and college campuses, but also on the television screen by courting media coverage. The women's liberation movement gained international recognition when it demonstrated at the annual Miss America beauty pageant. The environmental movement, which evolved from the anti-nuclear movement, can trace its beginnings back to the protests of 1968. [The Stonewall riots, which marked the beginning of the Gay Rights movement occurred in 1969.]

Student Protests

Students from Harvard, Radcliffe, and Boston University held a four-day hunger strike to protest the Vietnam War. Students from all five public high schools in East L.A. walked out of their classes protesting against unequal conditions in Los Angeles Unified School District high schools. Over the next several days, they inspired similar walkouts at fifteen other schools.

New York University (NYU) students demonstrated against Dow Chemical because the company was the principal manufacturer of napalm, used by the U.S. military in Vietnam. Students at Columbia University protested the school's allegedly racist policies, three school officials were taken hostage for 24 hours.

> **Where do you see examples of postmodern thinking today?**

4

Picture This

"Tell me one last thing," said Harry. "Is this real? Or has this been happening inside my head?

Dumbledore beamed at him, and his voice sounded loud and strong in Harry's ears even though the bright mist was descending again obscuring his figure.

"Of course it is happening inside your head, Harry, but why on earth should that mean that it is not real?"

J.K. Rowling. Harry Potter and the Deathly Hallows

The Human Imagination

The human capacity to imagine, to hold representations of reality in our minds, sets us apart. We are aware of our surroundings in a way that other species on our planet cannot be. We interpret. We have an innate need to do this; we need to understand. We carry a deep longing for an explanation of what a thing is and more importantly why it is. And why is the question that only religion can answer. The religious imagination is a window to eternity, and yet it is so easy for finite things to block this vision.

In 1993, no publisher believed that a story told by an unnamed person, who travels all over Peru tracking down ancient manuscripts containing secrets both the church and the government were trying to suppress, would attract a substantial following. James Redfield was forced to publish it himself. *The Celestine Prophecy,* gripped the imagination of those lucky enough to get a copy from a friend, who had gotten it from a friend. Eventually it was picked up by Time Warner Books and enjoyed a respectable stay on the New York Times Bestseller List. The story which tells of the recovery of these ancient secrets, which were supposedly written in 600 BCE, unfolds slowly. Each secret is revealed only as the narrator experiences each of the nine "insights." Step by step, they build a case for how we are called to live as true human "beings."

What does this all really mean? The "truth" of Redfield's text, even though its story is classified as a work of fiction, created excitement and generated enthusiasm, if not a genuine change of perception, both in its characters and its readers. The power of the imagination was stirred by this "discovery from the past." Whether the work is original fiction or the reinterpretation of a sacred tradition, there is tremendous wisdom, power, and authority attributed to voices which speak to us "from the past." This was especially true during times of great social upheaval and moral uncertainty, as the Bible was losing its prominent place in much of Western society.

The imagination creates the possibility of seeing a world different from our world, or our world from a different perspective. Science fiction, fantasy novels and fairy tales are not just entertainment. They invite us to places beyond our usual understanding of reality. They pierce the walls of what is, in order to expose a deeper sense of truth. *Believing is seeing* is much more accurate, despite what the more popular cliché, *seeing is believing,* claims. We must be open to the possible existence of the new or the different, before we can see it, not the other way around. We see what we expect to see. Actually, once we have determined who you are or what you're up to, we have no further need to look at you more carefully, we know it all.

Everyone has a particular approach to reality. The mind defends the structure we have already created, or has been created for us by our culture; because we think that this is reality. If asked, we live this way because of our intentional choices. But the real cause of our behavior lies in our imagination. It is in and through images and emotions that we come to know the truth. The language our imagination uses to envision our reality is likely to be as ambiguous as the experiences that gave rise to our perceptions. Often our deepest truth can only be spoken of by using metaphor: it was like ... or it seemed as if ...

Einstein said that imagination is more important than knowledge. It forms "new images" in the mind that have not previously been experienced with the help of what we already know, have already seen or heard. It leads us to deeper and deeper truth. Sometimes it takes a movie or a novel, some form of real drama to get under our radar and pierce our preconceived notions of how the world works. A different worldview removes a bit of our blind spot; whole new vistas open up before our eyes. Once we're intrigued, there is something in the human spirit that searches for the answer which lies just beyond our grasp, or listens for a message from some secret, spiritual source.

The power of the symbols and metaphors we use to portray our experiences are real, whether they are factual or fictional. They persist in our imagination and influence our religious devotion, our moral behavior, as well as our social and political commitments. As we reflect on the images we experience, as we unpack, analyze, criticize, and explain them, we are creating a worldview, a personalized approach to the other, our deep-seated "meaning system." Creating a meaning system is human work. It has both a critical and a constructive task.

The only way to enlarge this system is to recognize the finiteness of the doctrines and dogmas of our culture and open ourselves to other possibilities. The way we explain the phenomena that grip our imagination mediates reality and focuses the vision of our entire society. All that we see and hear, but more importantly, how we interpret it creates a world, our world. Our perception of the world has a much greater effect on us than do the actual events that occur. We always see more than meets the eye; we experience everything through our meaning system. Nothing exists without content and context.

What we imagine, what we picture in our minds barely resembles actual experience. Especially when we are dealing with values, it is important to remember that we interpret more than we report. The imagination not only gives form to human experience, it redescribes reality. The stories we tell, the images we cling to, are formed by what makes sense to us. We are able to face the ambiguity of life because we

have framed a context that holds our meaning in a way that gives us hope.

There are questions that cannot be answered, important questions about who we are and what things mean. Yet we must and do answer them. Darwin noticed the pattern in the evolution of all that that exists; but could not tell us why it happened or how this universe came to be. We don't know; yet we desperately want to know. We need to know because we are meaning-seeking creatures. Our spirits are not satisfied without context. The gifts we posses as humans, our capacity to understand and to imagine, demand answers. What's it all about? What does it all mean? This yearning accounts for the popularity of Redfield's novels. We need answers.

From earliest times, humans told each other stories. Most of them dealt with our relationships to the spirits who controlled nature. Who are we? Who are they? How can we get them to protect us, or at least not harm us? These stories became a sort of sacred protection. The holy ones would travel into the spirit world and come back with explanations and directions for us to follow. Those who could commune with the spirits assured us we were not alone. If the right connections were made, if all promises were kept, if we behaved in a certain way, we would be safe.

What we knew, thousands of years ago, seems lost in our modern world. The rational, scientific worldview has summarily dismissed whatever could not be seen as "not real." Great material progress was made. But we are beginning to see that this is only half the deck. For many good reasons, and some not so good, our spiritual insights were ridiculed and even ignored. Spiritual beings are still seen by some as figments of our imagination. Forgetting their true power, our sacred stories, the great myths of civilization, are treated as old-fashioned fairy tales. They are merely make-believe tales for children.

Myths are about gods; legends are about heroes, and fairy tales are about woodcutters and princesses. All are essential to our psyche. Myths are deeply serious insights about divine-human interactions. They are expressed in highly imaginative narratives that contain profound truths that cannot be verified. We are incapable of explaining our relationship with the One Who Is Mystery; yet we need something solid to hold onto in the face of uncertainty. Myths can't be factual; so how can they be true? That's the problem. We're applying modern thought to premodern experience. So, why do we bother to grapple with myths?

They are true explanations of invisible realities which cannot be explained, yet they provide the meaning we desperately need. Just because we imagine something doesn't make it *imaginary* in the sense of being untrue. They are true and do not deceive us. Myths express the deepest longings of our subconscious. Truth lies deeper than fact, which, in its finiteness distorts full meaning.

Joseph Campbell devoted his life to restoring our respect for myth. He reminded a skeptical world that myths determine how and why and to what degree people value things. They create an intricate set of interlocking stories, rites, and customs that inform and give the pivotal sense of meaning and direction to a person, family, community, or culture. We will not understand or appreciate their power, he told us, unless we allow symbols to touch our subconscious. In 1949, Joseph Campbell published *The Hero with a Thousand Faces* where he introduced the idea that all mythic narratives are variations of a single great story.

The most important question Carl Jung asked his patients was, "What myth are you living?" Most people found it very difficult to answer this question. It is to our subconscious, which makes up about ninety percent of our perceptions, that myths speak. Myths are considered true if they are effective in establishing and holding our meaning system. So, whether we are aware of it or not, we have a story that directs our life. In the premodern Western world, it came from the Bible. That is no longer the case in many Western countries.

Fortunately, we are recovering our sense of the mysterious in our post-postmodern, quantum world. Today even our scientists have experienced the real presence of mystery in the universe. We must allow a deeper sense of both religion and science to emerge, if we expect to deal with the complexity and conflict that permeate our world.

The Western Myth

In the Bible, the first thee chapters of Genesis tell us who human beings are and what their relationship with God should be. The story gives two different explanations of how the world was created, gives us a glimpse of how our relationship with God should be, and tells us why the human condition is so difficult. Because of the actions of our first parents, the world is filled with sin and suffering.

> *In the beginning God created the heavens and the earth. . . God created the world in six days and rested on the seventh, the Sabbath day.*
>
> *Humans are created in the image and likeness of God and given domination over the rest of the world.*
>
> *God breathed life into the clay of the earth and created a living being, Adam. From Adam's rib, woman was created by God. They lived in the Garden of Eden their every need met.*
>
> *God told Adam and Eve to take care of the garden, but not to eat of the fruit of the Tree of the Knowledge of Good and Evil.*
>
> *The devil tempted Eve to use her own judgment and eat it anyway. He told her that if they ate the fruit they would be like God. Eve saw that the tree was attractive and the fruit looked good, so she ate some and so did Adam who was with her. What they learned was that they were naked.*
>
> *When God found out what they had done, he punished them. He told Adam he would have to work very hard for his food all his life and return to dust when he died. Eve's punishment was that she would have intense pain in childbirth and that she would be subject to her husband.*
>
> *Even though God threw them out of the garden and set an angel to guard against their return, God showed he still cared by making clothes for them before they left.*
>
> *All of humanity descended from this first couple. We struggle to remain faithful to God even though we have all been wounded by this original sin.*

Wait a minute! Before you dismiss this myth as untrue, or irrelevant, or naïve, think of the impact this one story has had on the Western world. These few passages are still quoted to explain and justify or condemn the beliefs and behavior of billions of people. This version of human creation has permeated our culture for two thousand years.

Some people even defy science and demand that this story be taught as science. A very similar story is written in the Qur'an. Muslims also look to this God and these stories for guidance and have used them as moral imperatives since they were revealed/written. Remember, the truth lies in the underlying meaning. Science can and has proved that the world has evolved; but it cannot tells us why. It is the province of religion to deal with why it exists and what the proper role the human species plays as a part of it.

In Our Right Mind: Right /Left Brain

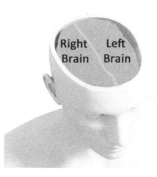

The brain is divided down the middle into two hemispheres, with each half performing a fairly distinct set of operations. Much of what is known about brain function is owed to Roger Sperry, whose experiments examined the way the human brain's hemispheres operate, both independently and in concert with each other. The two hemispheres communicate information, such as sensory observations, to each other through the thick corpus callosum that connects them.

The brain's right hemisphere controls the muscles on the left side of the body, while the left hemisphere controls the muscles on the right side. Because of this criss-cross wiring, damage to one side of the brain affects the opposite side of the body.

The **left hemisphere** processes information sequentially in a linear orderly fashion. It builds a hierarchy of categories for evaluating and judging reality. It controls and directs consciousness, abstracting pieces of information from the whole. Logic, reasoning, critical thinking, speech, verbal behavior, reading, writing, and remembering names are directed by left brain activity, which dominates modern thinking.

The **right hemisphere** processes information more diffusely and indirectly, integrating material in a simultaneous, holistic manner. It synthesizes parts to form a whole. Unconscious inner focus, art, music, recognizing faces, expressing emotions, dreaming, intuition, imagination, creativity, and spirituality are right brain activities, which is extremely active in young children and has been recovered in the postmodern world.

Note: Myth, the product of human creativity, imagination and spirituality resides in the right brain. Its truth is based on an intuitive understanding of the world. The left brain cannot logically analyze it, or prove its facticity, nor can it disprove it, for that matter. This is one of the major conflicts between religion, based on the mythic expression of a people's experience, and science.

5

What Do You Think
You're Doing?

*It is easier to judge an alien culture than to understand it. We tend
to look at things through the filters of our own racial and cultural
biases. Are we capable of reaching out and, if we do are we capable of
comprehension?*
— *excerpt from a Bene Gesserit report on galactic settlements*

Frank Herbert. Paul of Dune

We Always Did It This Way!

Our innate social nature leads us to gather with others in relationship.
This is one of the reasons our species has survived, when earlier humans without this skill became extinct. Society enables its members to
benefit in ways that would not otherwise be possible on an individual basis. Living together requires cooperation and clear expectations
of proper behavior, especially in the areas of economics and politics.
While all societies create specific social, political and economic systems, they are expressed in different ways among each group of people
depending on surrounding circumstances.

The assumptions, accumulated beliefs and practices of a group filter its perceptions of life, creating a culture that determines how its
members live in the world. Our parents and our culture interpret and
give meaning to our lives until we are capable of doing so for our-

selves. But even when we come to know that we know, there is still a vast amount of data, buried deep in our subconscious, that influences our judgment, because we always did it this way it feels like the right thing to do.

Every aspect of society, how we interact, what we wear, how we educate our children, how we punish misbehavior, is established by our culture. Our myth, our story, and the way our ancestors lived it

set the basic pattern. They, of course, were very wise in their decision-making, the way they chose is the perfect way for humans to live. Any group that acts differently than we do must be wrong. We assume our assumptions are the right ones.

These cultural assumptions anchor our worldview, let us know how to relate to others, and give us a strong sense of belonging. It is so clear that we're right and any other way of being is stupid or evil. We have been so formed by the expectations surrounding us that we rarely question their validity. Those among us who advocate for change are viewed with suspicion and marginalized. The vehemence of our current political campaigns indicates how some issues are held to be untouchable. We see the world correctly, and they don't!

Differences of opinion, changing lifestyles and even the evolution of how basic principles are expressed, should promote debate. When they challenge deep, unconscious values, they can provoke conflict and bitter recrimination. People, whose wordviews are at different levels of consciousness, are **incapable** of seeing the values of one another. Even when we are really trying to understand each other, our faithfully held view of what it means to be an American or Christian or human being, blocks our capacity to admit any other way of life as valid. Often the issues we argue about mask the fact that it is our underlying value systems that are diametrically opposed. Conversation becomes impossible.

We are made for culture and by culture. It is dynamic, in that it changes as its members change; but usually this happens at a very slow pace. Some individuals within the culture, especially the less connected, change more quickly. But because culture is essentially invisible, and its basic assumptions predominantly unconscious, the phrase "But we always did it this way!" usually ends any conversation about change, and the different is ignored, ridiculed or outright rejected.

Culture is not a thing; it is an invisible, unconscious force that directs our beliefs, priorities, our core values. The left-brain focuses on how to act and what our traditions are, things explicitly taught. But ninety percent of culture is subconscious. Learned behavior is assimilated and assigned meaning without full awareness of its implications. This deeper meaning of our lives is implicitly stored by our right brain. When one-half of the brain dominates, our perceptions are skewed in that direction.

Modern society prides itself on the human capacity to reasonably order our lives. Recently this belief has been challenged. The metaphor that Jonathan Haidt uses in his book, *The Happiness Hypothesis*, compares the left brain to a rider on the back of an elephant. While the rider may presume superiority and control, the elephant cannot be controlled by force or by logic. As we saw earlier, only if an elephant has been "conditioned" to certain behavior, activity which takes place in the emotional right brain, will it obey the prodding of the rider. Intuitions come first. Our early childhood conditioning to what is YUMMY and what is YUCKY, another image Haidt uses, sets the pattern of our lives.

The rider's job is to serve the elephant; yet the rider's input can substantially improve the elephant's life. Reason has and does make a huge contribution to human happiness. Perhaps its greatest contribution is in enabling us to surface some of those initial YUMS and YUCKS, and see if they still serve us as we face new situations. The basic change needed is perceptual. Reason justifies what we believe; finding our voice means challenging those preconceived notions that trap us today in outdated assumptions.

It is extremely difficult to escape the power of our culture, as it lies deep within our psyche. When an element of culture is called into question, if our only frame of reference is the culture itself, it is very difficult to judge it objectively. Spiral Dynamics shows how we must look to a higher worldview to solve the earlier worldview's problems. This new consciousness will grow eventually into a new cultural perspective.

The House

Once upon a time three little pigs each built a house. The first house was built of straw, the second of wood, and the third of brick. When the little girl found the house she was so glad, because she had been walking a long distance through the forest. She was tired, cold and hungry. She opened the door and saw three chairs at the table. The first chair was too high, the second too low, but the third was just right.

On the table were three bowls of porridge. She ate the one that was just right. When the three bears found her in the just-right-bed, Goldilocks ran away screaming. Just then the wolf came and told the pigs that he was going to huff and puff and blow the house down. He did blow the first house down and the first pig ran to the second house.

The dwarfs tried to protect Snow White; but they had to go to work. They told her not to open the door for anyone. When the woman selling apples appeared so upset, Snow White felt sorry for her. She let her in and bought one of her apples. When Snow White bit into the apple, she fell into a deep sleep. The pigs thought they were safe in the wooden house; but when the wolf came, he huffed and he puffed and the house came down.

The two homeless pigs ran to the house made of brick. The wolf tried to blow the house down but he couldn't, so he went away. The pigs were so happy. While the wolf was walking in the woods, he met a young girl on the way to her grandmother's house. She was wearing a red cape and carrying a basket full of gifts. The wolf took a short-cut and got to the house before the little girl could and ate her grandmother.

When Little Red Ridinghood got to the house she thought her grandmother looked and acted very strange. When the wolf jumped out of the bed and tried to eat her too, she screamed. A woodman heard her and came to her rescue. He cut the wolf open, so grandma could escape. He bent over and kissed the Sleeping Beauty. She woke up immediately. And they all lived happily ever after.

Perspective

Interpretation: Because we are familiar with the fairytales that are used, we know that while house occurs in each of them, completely different stories have been woven together. Those who don't know the tales would read a rather disjointed story about wolf and a woman whose name keeps changing.

The Hebrew Bible was written during different times of crisis, each of which caused the "Chosen People's" understanding of God to evolve. When these stories were merged we ended up with a rather disjointed story; pieces that were true at one point were moved beyond at others, and we can't be sure which is which.

THE DIVINE

6

OMG: wru?

"Do the gods of different nations talk to each other? Do the gods of Chinese cities speak to the ancestors of the Japanese? To the lords of Xibalba? To Allah? Yahweh? Vishnu? Is there some annual get-together where they compare each other's worshippers? Mine will bow their faces to the floor and trace wood grain lines for me, says one. Mine will sacrifice animals, says another. Mine will kill anyone who insults me, says a third. Here is the question I think of most often: Are there any who can honestly boast, My worshipers obey my good laws, and treat each other kindly, and live simple and generous lives?"

Orson Scott Card. Children of the Mind

OMG: Oh, my God! Almost everyone uses this phrase. God is invoked in circumstances that range from prayerful praise to outrage, in our moments unbelief and even in physical ecstasy, we say, Oh, my God! Instinctually we call on the highest power, the most intimate force to witness what is happening to us.

wru? OMG may be perhaps universally recognized but "wru" might mean many things.
God . . .

Who? What? Where? Why? [as well as many other "w" words] are you?

Picture This

There is a story told of a young girl who was never really engaged in school. One day during art class she was diligently drawing at her desk. She seemed so focused and determined that the teacher asked her what she was drawing. "I am drawing a picture of God," she replied. The teacher told her that no one knows what God looks like. "They will when I'm finished," she replied confidently.

How do you picture God? Take a moment and write down your answers.

- Do you imagine God as a super male being, or as a strict or a loving parent?
- Is God to be feared?
- Does God have a special plan for each of us?
- Is God a policeman in the sky?
- Does God watch and judge our every thought and action?
- What does God want of us?
- Does God really exist?
- How often does God forgive us?
- Does God hear and answer our prayers?
- Is God on our side?

When an interviewer asked Neale Donald Walsch, the author of several books describing his *Conversations with God*, if he could sum up briefly what God wants to say to the world, he immediately replied, "You've got me all wrong." He explains his answer in his most recent book, *God's Message to the World*. Judging from current world conditions, Neale concludes as many do, that none of the systems we humans, have put in place are working very well. Since most of our traditions are based on the early rules and laws of some faith tradition, and all of our moral codes derive from the mandates of religion, should we consider the fact that our moral culture has been seriously wounded by our mistaken beliefs in God?

What we have is a picture of an Infinite Being drawn by a finite culture. Of course that is the best we can do. No matter how awesome the experience, we are limited by the level of our consciousness. When the left brain speaks it cannot fully explain what has captured our hearts. Yet we do speak, even though words fail. The problem arises when we forget that only symbols and metaphor touch the rich images of our right brain. What we need is a new cultural story that remembers and relates to God as mystery. How can we allow our right-brained voice to be heard?

The concept of God is beyond human comprehension. We know that to define "God" is impossible. Yet we continue to invoke and describe who he or she or they are, as if we could. "God" is the answer to all the questions with which our myths grapple. We, who need meaning, find it in that place that lies beyond us, and for theists, at least, in the One who is Ultimate Meaning, our Higher Power.

God is the deepest, richest, most profound mystery imaginable. Western culture, as we have seen, begins with human beings being created in God's image. As we talk about that which cannot be imagined, we actually do just that. Just as we solve for the x in an algebraic problem, we search our minds and hearts for a way to express this power, this presence that we sense all around us. So, in fact, we have and we continue to create God in our image. It's the best we can do, and it is usually helpful as long as "God" grows, or our understanding of God grows, as our consciousness does. This, we will see, is a very difficult thing to do.

Most people will concede the inadequacy of human words to accurately describe "God" and will allow that "God" is mystery. "God" is beyond human imagination. "God" is beyond human comprehension. Yet when it comes to our daily lives, most people proceed as if they know who God is and what "he" wants in great detail!

Let me repeat that. GOD IS SO FAR BEYOND HUMAN COMPREHENSION that any image we use is woefully inadequate. We, however, can't exist without meaning, so we must create God in our image. When we look at how the various levels of consciousness describe Ultimate Meaning, we see that they were limited by the stage of development to which their culture had evolved. The best a warrior culture can do is to see God as the Ultimate Warrior. Traditional culture envisions the Ultimate Lawgiver. This was the highest expression possible at the time. As culture matures and becomes more complex, so should its understanding of God and what God expects.

Western egalitarianism has allowed all levels of consciousness a forum. Today, as we shall see, the entire spectrum of humanity's relationship with the Divine flourishes in some part of the world. Those who take Clare Grave's leap into Integral Consciousness will be the first to respect these differences. Those who haven't will fight to preserve their revered image of God, forgetting that it is culture-bound and woefully inadequate. OMG, what do you think of this?

History of God in Western Culture

Early tribal life revolved around honoring and influencing the spirits. Humans innately perceived that there were "powers" in the world that can't be seen. They were aware of "magic" surrounding them. This openness to the spiritual world brought some security in their otherwise short, brutal lives. These spirits became the "gods" of legend and myth.

"God" began as the spirits of the tree and the river, the protectors of the land, the bringers of good fortune, the avengers of misconduct. As human civilization developed so did our concept of the Divine. In the premodern Western World, "God" became the Creator, the Redeemer, the Infinite, the Almighty, the Ultimate, and the All-Powerful. How do you describe "God"?

"God" is the generic word we use to explain the Great Creator / Mover of the universe. The God encountered in the Bible has dominated Western imagination and myth since the last days of the Roman Empire. According to the Bible, the foundation of meaning for the premodern Western world, humans have been made in God's image, and our culture was clear on what that meant. These myths, supported by a Judeo-Christian understanding of God, have formed our institutions and our consciences if not our constitutions for centuries. We have responded to this God in many different ways, from many different perspectives.

Yet in Europe and North America, for the last half century, culture no longer blindly supports religion, in fact, in many cases religion and society are diametrically opposed to one another. The problem is that since we no longer share a sense of who "God" is, we can't agree on who we are. Somewhere in the 1970s, the religious foundation of Western culture was rejected by half the population. Modern culture decided we could take care of ourselves. And the existential questions of the postmodern era could no longer be answered as easily as they could when the Bible and church teaching were accepted without question, and we "knew" God. If we cannot know who God is, where does that leave us?

Organized religion, as we know it, continues to struggle with the mythic questions, trying to make sense of life. Many today claim to be spiritual but not religious. Still others claim to be neither. Whether we need new answers or new questions may be argued. But when we lost our common understanding of who, what, where, or why God is, we lost the collective sense of ourselves, our fundamental meaning system. No wonder we're fragmented.

The Breaking Story:
A Model for Integral Religion

T his just in . . .

A young girl breaks into the three bears' home while they are away.
She eats and sleeps there until the bears return home.
The girl then flees; leaving the bears to estimate the damage done.

Everyone is talking about what happened. Time and Newsweek ran special editions on runaway children. There were ads posted by The Just Right Furniture Company and its subsidiary, The Just Right Oatmeal Company. Slomin's Shield has offered discount prices on home security systems.

Articles appeared in the following newspapers and magazines:

Criminal Justice Magazine
MS Magazine
Animal Right's Quarterly
Parents' Magazine
Child Welfare Society Bulletin
House Beautiful
Better Homes and Gardens
National Wildlife Magazine
Psychology Today
Wall Street Journal
Outdoor Life
National Parks Magazine
The National Enquirer
Newsday

What do you think the gist of each article was?

Perspective

Interpretation: Because of the varied interests of the editors and readers of the different periodicals, the story appears from a different perspective in each. Each publication emphasized different points and drew very diverse conclusions, without violating the "facts" of the story. Religion also has its own slant on current events.

THE RELATIONSHIP

7

The Eye of the Beholder,
The Heart of the Believer

You told me, God made the World.

No, no! I told you that, while all these many religions said many things, most of them said, God made the World. I do not grok* the fullness, but that 'God' was the word that was used.

Yes, Jubal," Mike agreed. "Word is 'God'" He added. "You grok."

"No, I must admit I don't grok." "You grok," Smith repeated firmly. "I am explain. I did not have the word. You grok. Anne groks. I grok. The grass under my feet groks in happy beauty.

But I needed the word. The word is God."

Jubal shook his head to clear it. "Go ahead."

Mike pointed triumphantly at Jubal. "Thou art God!"

> *Robert Heinlein.* Stranger in a Strange World

What is Religion?

St. Irenaeus, a doctor of the early church, taught that the glory of God is the human person fully alive. And that the vocation of the human person is to see God. How we "see" God is determined by our world-view. The Ultimate Mystery, infinite in itself, is experienced differently at each level of consciousness. It's not that we won't see God any other

---

* *Grok means to understand so thoroughly that the observer becomes a part of the observed — to merge, blend, lose identity in group experience.*

way. We experience God in and through our human cultural context. We **can't** see further than our capacity allows.

Religion is derived from three Latin words *religio* meaning, the fear or awe one feels in the presence of spirit or god, *religare*, which means to tie fast or bind together, and *relegere* which means to reread, to bind, to rethink. What is it that binds us together with this Awesome Presence and with each other? Relationship is the key word. Our identity is formed in and by relationships. What is the essence of the human relationship with the divine? How has our understanding of this relationship shifted through time and space? What happens to the human expression of this relationship in different contexts? In different cultures?

The answers to these questions shape our understanding of religion understood as the public expression of our relationship with the divine. Just as our relationships with parents, friends and lovers change as we grow as individuals. To remain relevant religion must rearticulate its understanding of the divine-human covenant as we mature. We will examine how the different levels of consciousness "picture" God in Part Four; here we are dealing with the concept itself.

The business of religion is the construction, evaluation, and reconstruction of our understanding of God and the development of a specific meaning system which describes our obligations because of this relationship. Those who believe that there is a Being who directs or controls the order of the universe, commit themselves to following the will of this "God." The constant challenge is to articulate, and more importantly to re-articulate this experience as human culture evolves, and calls forth greater complexity. We cannot confuse the expression with the relationship.

The human capacity for hope and surprise, our curiosity, our need for deep meaning, our need for community and our sense of disconnection from that very community, pulls us toward relationship with God. Religion demands our surrender, our submission to that which is greater. It provides a place to belong, and a compass, which gives us a clear path to follow. Any authority figures, social structures and cultural practices that enable us to be a part of this group are legitimized. Safety and fulfillment come from the knowledge that our participation honors the Sacred One and the confidence that of our fidelity will be rewarded.

Before we attempt a definition, let's look at some of the factors involved. We're talking about human involvement in the realm of the sacred. Although it is expressed in thought and action; in essence religion is a function of the human spirit. More specifically, it expresses our connection with that which we are not. Ambiguity and fear generate a need for safety. William James believed that all religion begins with a cry, a cry for help.

God is the object of our concern. Our image of God can be expressed only by using metaphors and symbols. I am using the term religion generically to mean our basic value system. This value system, whether it connects with a specific organized religion or not, flows from how we perceive the Divine and what we consider to be the ultimate meaning of life. The collection of the stories, beliefs and practices that surface as we develop these images serves as the ultimate reference point for understanding everything in the world around us.

The particular myth we accept as the correct way, the holy way, the only way in some cases, to salvation permeates our lives. It is the source of our moral code, the measure of promised reward, our very connection with all that is. It also tells us what to expect after death. We are committed to follow its directives with every fiber of our beings. No wonder it is so so difficult to rearticulate the image as we move to a new level of consciousness.

The inherent flaw in religion is that it can forget that myths are symbolic, poetic, imaginative narratives. The truth they hold is beyond human comprehension. New consciousness demands new images. So often the images we hold on to, or cling to, for that matter, harden into cultural assumptions and "definitive" doctrines that cannot and must not be changed. This is a clear indication that something has been lost. Once religion hardens into a set of specific rules and customs it should more properly be called a belief system. It is not a specific definition of the Deity but a living, growing relationship that must be maintained.

What has been lost is a sense of mystery. One widely accepted [finite] definition of religion characterizes it as a system of beliefs and rituals related to the Holy. While this mentions the Holy, the emphasis usually focuses on what its adherents do, and loses the sense of relationship with Mystery. James Carse calls belief systems finite expressions of an ideology. An Integral [infinite] definition of religion sees it as a collective response to Mystery that can be expressed in many ways; but cannot survive without this sense of being present to Infinite

Mystery.

The major difference is one of certitude. Belief systems completely explain every area of our relationship with God. There is little room for doubt or opposition. True religion is full of questions. It constantly brings us face-to-face with the mystery of life and offers the assurance that we are in intimate relation with "God" who calls us to be more fully human in ever changing ways.

Mystical experience, direct awareness of God's presence, provides the seed. A person or group who experienced the Holy so vividly could not help but tell others about it. These stories became myths. By retelling and reliving the experience, others joined in and owned it for themselves. Every year, at Passover, every Jew says, "I was in Egypt and you rescued me." On Good Friday, Christians are asked, "We're you there when they crucified my Lord?"

The enthusiasm generated in sharing the experience forms a vibrant community. The people joyously and communally respond to the Mystery. Without the heart, without right-brained engagement with art, music, and dance, without true celebration that is very much aware of the Divine Presence, the intellect, the left brain is left to define who God is. Without meeting the Holy One and being caught up in wonder and awe, religion becomes an empty shell.

If we wish to truly be present to the mystery that is God, to be in relationship with the One who calls us, we must constantly rethink and rearticulate what this relationship means. We must allow our image of God to change as we "the created image of God" grow and change for better and for worse. As we continue into the twenty-fist century many rejoice at having recovered this insight.

Others are so committed to their sense of church, or temple or mosque, so threatened and disillusioned by the disorder and irreverence of modern culture, that they reject any attempt at change in religious thought or practice. And to be fair, many of these traditional believers have never lost a sense of God's presence in their midst.

The Games We Play

In *Finite and Infinite Games: A Vision of Life as Play and Possibility*, James Carse, introduced the concept of infinite games. Infinite games have no end in their design, the fundamental commitment is to keep the game in play. He contrasts this with the more traditional view of the world that sees life as a series of discrete encounters, each to be won or lost, with a final scoreboard at the end that sums up the success or failure of our existence.

If a finite game is to be won by someone, it must come to a definitive end. It will come to an end when someone has won. Winning is determined by the agreement of the players. A finite game has a precise beginning and end, and has clear spatial and numerical boundaries. There must be at least one opponent. In a finite game there can be only one winner, but other players may be ranked at the end of play.

Infinite games are the opposite in every way. They have no spatial, temporal, or numerical boundaries, and no winners or rankings. They have no discernible beginning or ending. The goal is to keep playing. Finite games can be played within an infinite game, but no infinite game can be played within a finite game.

Another way to look at an infinite game is to see it as a journey rather than a destination. Carse describes the effect apocalyptic thinking, with its finite focus on the end-times, has had on religion, ecology and politics. The alternative approach, commitment to keeping history alive and evolving offers hope in an uncertain world. If we can move away from ideology and allow ourselves to be surprised by wonder, there will be less need for confrontation and more room for growth.

	Finite Games / Players	Infinite Games / Players
Examples	card games, games of chance, sports, receiving a degree Politics: litigation / the war on terror / superpowers	evolution, life, love Social vision: justice / 'diplomacy' / global order
Rules	fixed rules and boundaries – may not be broken or changed	unknown and shifting rules and boundaries
Arena	Society: try to fix the future based on the past	Culture: meaning of the past changes depending on what happens in the future
Manner of play	theatrical – follow script – dread of unpredictable	dramatic – no script – each moment a new [playful] choice
Preparation	trained [prepared against surprise]	educated [prepared for surprise]

Questions: Are you aware of the game you're playing? Does it make a difference? Is religion a finite or an infinite game?

Basic Resources for Part Two

Armstrong, Karen. *A Short History of Myth*. New York: Canongate US, 2006.

Campbell, Joseph. *The Hero with a Thousand Faces*. Princeton University Press, 1973.

_____. *Thou Art That: Transforming Religious Metaphor*. Novato, CA: New World Library, 2013.

Carse, James. *Finite and Infinite Games: A Vision of Life as Play and Possibility*. New York: Free Press, 1986.

_____. *The Religious Case against Belief.* New York: Penguin Books, 2008.

Carson, Rachel. *Silent Spring.* New York: Houghton Mifflin, 1962.

Darwin, Charles. *The Origin of the Species.* New York: Signet, 2003.

Haidt, Jonathan. *The Happiness Hypothesis.* New York: Basic Books, 2006.

Redfield, James. *The Celestine Prophecy: An Adventure.* New York: Warner Books, Inc., 1997.

Rolston, Holmes III. *Three Big Bangs: Matter-Energy, Life, Mind.* New York: Columbia University Press, 2010

Walsch, Neale Donald. *God's Message to the World: You've Got Me All Wrong.* Faber, VA:

Rainbow Bridge Books, 2014.

Part III

AFAICS
[As Far as I Can See]

The Theories

8

Where Do You Think You're Going?

Spiral Dynamics

After the first chapter you were invited to look at the levels of consciousness that Clare Graves identified. In the ensuing chapters, we have looked how our humanity and our relationship to divinity has been expressed in Western Civilization. Now it's time to see where Graves' theory led and how it can be helpful in the twenty-first century.

Don Beck and Chris Cowan collaborated on a book, *Spiral Dynamics*, explaining Dr. Graves work; but after its publication in 1996, their work took them in different directions. My research follows Don Beck who focuses on facilitating cultural transformation using the insights of Spiral Dynamics. Donald Edward Beck, PhD, worked with Mandela and de Clerk in South Africa and is currently working with both Palestinians and Israelis in the Middle East. Large corporations and football teams have benefitted from his counsel, as well.

The framework of Spiral Dynamics remains indebted to Graves' original research: a way of thinking about human nature by increasing our understanding of **why** we do as we do. We are then able to broaden our conception of the choices we have in deciding what we might do next. The concept is based on the movement of human consciousness toward ever greater complexity. At each turn of the "spiral" an evolution of sorts takes place. Graves' predicted that each change in consciousness is accompanied by a chemical change in the brain. He identified the first few changes before his death in 1986.

The interaction of evolving life conditions, and the human capacity to adapt to them, inspire new insights that lead to deeper levels of consciousness. In most cases the new conditions are more complex than the former and the adaptation leads to a different, more complex intelligence better able to function in the new environment. In times of crisis, there is the temptation to regress to lower level values where we **were** comfortable and knew what to do, rather than grappling with the unknown challenge. But civilization depends on us evolving through the stages, so Spiral Dynamics can be seen as an infinite game.

Significant Factors to Note

The levels describe types *in* people not types *of* people. Once these levels have been manifested in human consciousness, we have evolved to level eight at the present moment, all future growth will follow this trajectory. The way the levels are expressed may differ; but the mindset, the worldview, the basic value system is set. Each level describes how a person thinks, not what is believed. Faithful, traditional Jews, Muslims and Christians are committed to following God's will, yet each community follows different rules and performs different rituals in doing so.

No one stage is inherently better or worse than any other. There is nothing intrinsically better about a thirty-two year old than there is about a three year old. Yet the behaviors of the two should differ significantly. If each is acting appropriately, each would be considered psychologically healthy. Of course, the adult is capable of more complex judgment because of his or her experience. But it is the age-appropriateness of the response to a given situation that is judged. The evolving complexity of life calls for continual maturation. We do not expect a person to be the same at three and thirty-two.

To solve the problems of one stage requires the worldview and skills of the next level of consciousness. Because of our innate desire for stability, when we find something that works, we are slow to give it up. More of the same, only better, is usually our first reaction when things don't work. What Spiral Dynamics shows is that when we are too successful at a given level, we are actually creating the life conditions that eventually will call for a new level, thus the spiral.

Each succeeding stage, as we have seen, alternates from accepting the world as it is and making peace with it by sacrificing self for the sake of community to expressing our new self-concept in an effort to fix what we perceive to be wrong. One has to experience the consciousness of each stage before moving on to the next level. However, those personalities that are more individualistic and relish self-expression will be more aware of the agentic expressive levels. The more communal minded will recognize and cherish the communal phases of the spiral.

All levels have both strengths and weaknesses. If a person or society doesn't evolve to the next level, the pathology or shadow side of the current level begins to show. When the life conditions which called forth the worldview have been addressed, the solution that was "perfect" becomes problematic. Cracks begin to appear. Discomfort, disappointments, and dissatisfaction are felt. New issues arise which call for new questions, not new answers to old questions. Yet our tendency is to hold on to what we know. We become fixated with the values of this particular level, oblivious to the damaging aspects that have arisen.

Integralists know that as we move from one stage to next nothing of significance is lost. The dynamic is to transcend and at the same time to include the gifts of the previous level. We continue to change but keep the best we have with us as we go forward. Having mastered the skills required to live today, we posses strengths that can be called upon whenever circumstances warrant. But today's tools won't work in tomorrow's world. The most difficult aspect of growth is that we may have to leave behind behaviors and beliefs that have become comfortable. Sacred traditions, meaningful exchanges, and the expectations of the community change. This, you may realize immediately, causes great resistance to accepting the "new."

Everyone is motivated but not by the same thing. If we recognize that one size doesn't fit all, we are able to speak to people, and society, in a way that they understand. By working with the driving forces that are important to them, we are more likely to be heard and perhaps to be understood. The theory holds that the healthy completion of one level naturally leads to the next. It is an inevitable, but slow, process.

Don Beck has said that Clare Graves once told him, "All you can do is help a country [or a person] become what is next for it to become. The belief that you can create this Utopian Vision, and with a sleight of hand you can turn it into heaven on earth, is not in the cards. What is in the cards is what is next for them. If you help them do that, nature will take care of you." He told Don that if you try to force change on people who are not ready for it, it will create a backlash.

Terminology

Meme: [rhymes with gene] a term introduced by Richard Dawkins who used it to describe a unit of cultural information. They self-reproduce, they interact with their surroundings and adapt to them, they mutate, they persist. They carry a perception of the world that infects surrounding belief systems and cultures. In essence, they act like viruses which can be transmitted from one mind to another through writing, speech, gesture, ritual or some other imitable phenomena.

^{v}MEME: Beck and Cowan use Dawkins' term designating a basic "^{value} meme system" associated with each level of consciousness identified by Clare Graves.

Memetic code: the recognition that the eight layers of human consciousness can be described by characteristics particular to each specific worldview. The ^{v}memes form a double helix pattern which determines societal identity just as the genetic code determines biological identity.

The Human Memome Project: directed by Don Beck. The Center for Human Emergence is developing a way to map the memetic codes (meshes of the stages or levels of consciousness) of the major peoples, drivers, institutions, movements, and organizations of the world, in order to create a synthesis of all of the various viewpoints on cultural transformation, societal change, the nature of conflict, forms of conflict prevention, and development.

The Stages: Humanity's Quest to Improve Life Conditions

Coping systems [bolded on the right] are generated to solve current Problems of Existence [on the left] as each stage becomes manifest in the course of a person's life, or through cultural evolution.

Problems of Existence   *Emergent Coping Systems*

First Tier: only capable of accepting one worldview at a time

1. SurvivalSense: INSTINCTUAL
Each day is a struggle to stay alive
    -> sharpen insights, join together in small bands

2. KinSpirits: MAGIC
Threatening world of many spirit beings and mysterious forces
    -> rely on chief, group, or magic to find safety and security for the people

3. PowerGods: TERRORISM
Power-driven in hostile world with strength as the key to staying alive
    -> depend on self, act impulsively and ruthlessly, break free

4. TruthForce: OBEDIENCE TO GOD'S LAW
Need for purpose, stability and order in life and a reason for death
    -> sacrifice now for the Truth that offers answers now and salvation later

5. StriveDrive: SELF-INTEREST AND SUCCESS
Sense possibility of movement to do better than others and to win
    -> use ingenuity and strategy to reach goals to better one's self and some others

6. Human Bond: EGALITARIAN – ALL TO BE TREATED EQUALLY
Recognize the inequality and damage caused by oppressive economic and dogmatic systems
    -> join others to build consensus and share feelings to make things better now for everyone

---

This is the step that Clare Graves envisioned.   A movement from dualism, where all other levels are misunderstood and mistrusted, to Integration, where one can see and hear the healthy aspects of each, it calls for "a momentous leap" where a chasm of unbelievable depth of meaning is crossed.

This can be seen as a second enlightenment or a correction on the insights of the first. What would have happened if religion and science had accepted each other's insights?

Second Tier: we see that each level of the spiral is critically important for the health of all.

Wider, deeper perspectives, motivated by love, not fear.

7. FlexFlow: WILLING TO WORK TO INTEGRATE AND ENABLE ALL LEVELS
Finds all systems lack complete answers for living in a highly complex world

> *-> integrate and align systems in search for the most functional way possible*

8. WholeView: HOLISTIC / MYSTICAL
Knows the Earth needs a coordinated approach to new global problems

> *-> cooperate with world-wide networks to address issues impacting all life forms*

Color My World

D on Beck insists that the problems in the world are not really about skin color, religion or whether we are conservative or liberal. He is convinced that, in essence, the differences that divide us reflect different levels of consciousness. The end of the Cold War and the rise in our sense of respect for human rights has allowed all the previous levels to resurface. In our permissive postmodern world ALL the levels have been granted a forum and are very much active.

Spiral Dynamics uses a color-coded short hand Don and Chris Cowan developed in the 1970s to designate the different levels. They replaced Clare Graves' lettering system with appropriate colors related to each level of consciousness. Each color represents a complete mind-set. [Originally Ken Wilber used these colors too; but he has shifted his coding to the electromagnetic spectrum.]

Beige: savanna grasslands [Early Bands]
Purple: the royal color of tribal chiefs and monarchs [Tribal]
Red: hot blooded emotions [Warlords]
Blue: the sky, the heavens, and the True [blue] Believer [Authoritarian Structures]
Orange: radiating energy of an industrial furnace [Pragmatic Materialists]
Green: grass, forests, and ecological consciousness [Sensitivity]
Yellow: solar power and alternative technologies [Integration]
Turquoise: the color of oceans on Earth as viewed from space [Connection]
[Coral: life deep within the seas - not yet emerging]

Don was able to relate the colors to specific groups of people when he worked in South Africa. Using the colors allowed them to focus on levels of consciousness not race, on deep rather than surface differences. Because of the great diversity in South Africa all the colors were very much present and all the levels had to be considered in any negotiations. The object was not to move them to different levels; but to present the problems in a way that spoke to the healthy aspects of each viewpoint.

Mandela's use of rugby to form a bond among South Africans, who otherwise had little in common, is an example of how this works. Instead of trying to change one group's thinking to conform with another's, the South Africans found something that gave them a sense of unity and pride. Much work still needs to be done; but by learning how to speak to and appreciate the different levels of consciousness we stand more of a chance of being heard. This can be done only after one achieves the FlexFlow, Yellow, Second Tier consciousness.

We all wear colored glasses. We all see things differently. Don Beck has found a way to get beneath surface differences and appeal at a level that can be understood, at each person's or group's level of consciousness.

9

Where Do You Belong: Integral Theory

Integral theory was developed by the philosopher, psychologist, and mystic, Ken Wilber. His greatest contribution to integral theory is his synthesis of human knowledge. Ken combined the best of pre-modern, modern, and postmodern reality, by chronicling the emergence of integral consciousness and culture in recent decades. Often referred to as a "theory of everything," integral theory allows us to see the patters that connect all the various dimensions of our lives, offering the most comprehensive and fully integrated view of reality that we have ever seen.

Over the last 30 years, Ken Wilber has taken literally everything that all the various cultures, disciplines, and methods have to tell us about human potential, about spiritual growth, psychological growth, and social growth and laid it out on a map: the Four Quadrant Map of the Kosmos. This map [See Figure 1] is usually referred to as AQAL, an acronym for all quadrants [all lines] and all levels. While it may seem daunting and complex, the beauty of it lies in its simplicity. Each quadrant represents one of the four basic perspectives by which an individual sees reality. The upper quadrants represent the individual; the lower the collective. The left quadrants chart interior growth and the right show exterior measurable behavior.

	Interior	Exterior
Individual	Intention I	Behavior It
Collective	We Culture	Its Social systems

Figure 1

The upper-left quadrant lays out the subjective first-person, "I", form of perspective. Individual intention, interior thoughts and motivation must be revealed by the subject and cannot be known unless it is. The lower-left quadrant tracks culture and collective intention. Culture, the composite of relationships among people, creates "we", the collective second-person dimension of human interaction. This is the domain where myth lives. It is also interior and outsiders have great difficulty understanding it. This is the realm of religion, morality, customs, values [Spiral Dynamics], and a variety of other cultural codes. The right quadrants measure exterior, measurable data, "It," that which we talk about in the third-person. The upper-right observes the physical behavior and development of individuals; and the lower-right studies social structures, forms of government, laws, etc. from an objective point of view.

The content of each quadrant lays out the various developmental stages of life, unfolds the spiral, so to speak, into lines, each moving toward greater complexity. Each stage on a line is considered a **holon**, an entity that is simultaneously a whole in and of itself and at the same time nested within another larger holon [the next stage of development] and so is also a part of something much more complex than itself. All the different **lines** of development are included: cognitive growth [Piaget], needs [Maslow], faith, [Fowler], values [Spiral Dynamics], spirituality, etc.

This classic graph shows the forms the various ᵛmeme codes in the different quadrants have taken through human history.

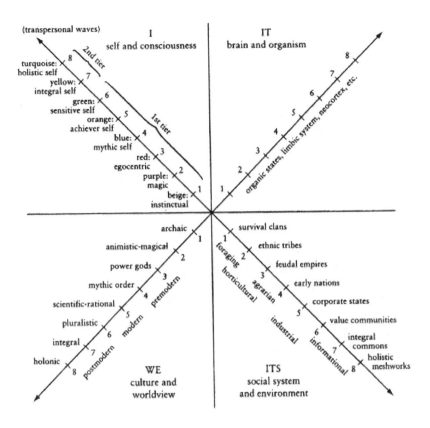

AQAL is comprised of just this handful of fundamental distinctions about reality itself. These distinctions are not just abstract notions; they can be located in our direct experience, and they concern the way we make sense of our life and world. But AQAL is a neutral framework; it does not tell us what to think, or force any particular ideologies on us, or coerce our awareness in any fashion, it just lays out the development. Precisely because AQAL is neutral, it can bring clarity to virtually any situation or topic.

Because the left side cannot be physically seen, intention and meaning must be interpreted. Surfaces can be seen; but consciousness must be perceived. One of the core insights of integral theory is just how significant perspective is in our universe. Our thoughts, relationships, behaviors, and interactions, are always filtered through our "current lens." We only "see" what our worldview permits. Everything is interpreted.

At the integral stage of development people are able to better, navigate, all the different perspectives, which brings the possibility of more wisdom, openness, and understanding than ever before. Because of its capacity for acknowledging the complexity of the post-postmodern world, the integral stage is the very first to honor and include the values of all the stages that have come before it. This does not mean that the integral stage provides answers, or even enough information to achieve adequate solutions. It merely recognizes the complexity and has the courage to begin to work with pieces of the problems we face.

The Big Three

Since they are both objective and can be seen and measured by the senses, Wilber conflated the quadrants on the right side, using "IT" to include both the individual and collective. He then associated the first, second and third person perspectives with what he calls the "big three" philosophical values of beauty, goodness, and truth. The UL first person quadrant represents the domain of beauty (which is deeply subjective), LL second person quadrant the domain of goodness (how we should act and treat each other), and right side third person the domain of truth, (that which is objectively verifiable). Before the Modern era, even the right side was assumed truth, believed but not provable. [See figure 2.]

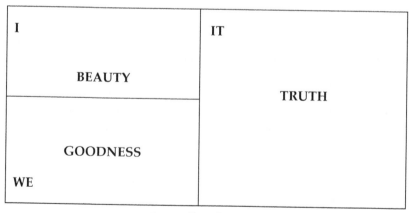

Figure 2

Steve McIntosh is a leader in the integral movement and the author of *Evolution's Purpose,* and *Integral Consciousness and the Future of Evolution,* as well as *The Presence of the Infinite,* to be published in the fall of 2015. He is currently the President and Co-Founder of the nonprofit social policy organization: The Institute for Cultural Evolution. He works to deepen our understanding of human consciousness and its implications for society. The institute has published several white papers applying integral theory to American politics and the crisis of extreme terrorism in the Middle East.

Steve's TED talk: "The Natural Theology of Beauty, Truth and Goodness" shows how these values play a central role in the evolution of the universe. Arguing that beauty, truth and goodness serve as attractors of evolutionary development pulling evolution forward through their influence on consciousness, he presents a master systemic plan to help us comprehend evolution more fully. Evolution is a two way street. The "evolved" are responsible to make things, as well as themselves better. "We" are also called to bring wisdom gained "down" to those on the lower levels so that they may see **their** level in its healthiest form.

Plato was the first writer to associate them; Kant used them as models for his critiques of reason; and Aurobindo saw them as "three dynamic images" through which one makes contact with "supreme Reality." They are considered transcendental, primary values on the grounds that everything that is is measured as true or false, good or evil, beautiful or ugly. Because we share a general sense of their meaning, we use these words in conversation and assume understanding. We cannot forget that each is articulated from a specific level of consciousness and means very different things at the different levels. As we look at each of the stages and its relationship to religion in Parts VI and V, clarified descriptions of these virtues [including justice] will offer us significant insight.

In his essay, "Social Transformation: Toward a More Just Kosmos," Joe Corbett, a critic of integral theory, argues against collapsing the right quadrants. Instead he would follow Jurgen Habermas' grammars of the four forms of life, which are the aesthetic-expressive (beauty), the moral-communal (goodness), the instrumental-technical (truth), **and strategic-political (justice)** forms of rationality that constitute human psychological, cultural, and social existence. Corbett believes that justice will be lost, if the right-hand quadrants are not kept separate.

I note this because justice cannot be ignored in the establishment of an integral world. Perhaps until recently justice was so embedded in our understanding of culture that it may have seemed unnecessary to single it out. Now, it seems that in the midst of the culture wars justice is often the first victim. Justice is already a constituent part of integral theory; it restoration is the focus of second tier worldviews. Truth easily encompasses justice, for what is justice, but a true sense of appropriate relationships. I will follow the classical philosophical tradition that Wilber used as the three values foundational to Western thought; but add a brief description of justice as perceived at each level.

Blinded by the Light

We don't like to be reminded, especially in public, of past childish behavior. One of the blessings of memory is that we do NOT remember the pitfalls of growing up. Those silly, nasty, embarrassing things we said and did are better off forgotten. The point is when I acted like a child, hopefully I was a child. There is a scene in *Sleepless in Seattle* when Noah is acting like a brat when Sam brings Victoria home. Sam merely says, "He's eight!" That seems to explain, if not excuse the behavior.

ᵛMemes, especially the first six, blind us. We are infected with worldviews that filter out, reject and ridicule all other realities. Because adults exist at every level of consciousness, Integral theory reminds us that adults can and do act like eight year old brats, when they haven't grown past that stage of consciousness.

When our level of consciousness matches the leading edge of our society's consciousness, we have matured to the highest level possible for that time and space. We fit. Life is YUMMY. But if our society operates at a level ahead, or behind us, we are usually threatened or repulsed by "their" behavior. **But they're acting according to their worldview! What else can they do? If we see the world differently, we act differently! So do they!**

This is crucial to remember as we look at the different levels in depth, particularly in the modern and postmodern cultures that predominate European and North American culture. We were eight once, and we don't like to be reminded of it! Other parts of the world have not yet been able to find the order and security necessary to embrace the next stages in their growth. And many of them look at our current chaos and refuse to let go of their certainties to join what they consider our disintegration.

To remind us of this, I end each level with this pattern:

Success generates the next problem: the core assumption that generated my acceptance of this worldview is challenged, disproven or outgrown; because its achievements have also exposed its limitations.

My dissatisfaction or disillusionment with my current perspective grows and as the **Shadow / Pitfalls/ Pathology** begin to surface, my world begins to **Crack!!!** There is more to life and I'm not sure if I am ready to face it.

If I can, if society can, I/we **Breakthrough:** to the awakening consciousness. But at the first six levels, what Spiral Dynamics calls the First Tier, we are blinded. Many are incapable of seeing this as a good thing. This leads to **Breakdown:** we cling to our slightly uncomfortable zone, viewing the next level as blasphemous, or evil. And those who have advanced, who have abandoned us, the "tried and true," are branded traitors. Those who have moved on look back at their previous worldview as immature, embarrassing, yes, even evil.

THE NEW BLOSSOM: THE NEXT ᵛMEME, our more complex understanding of God, religion, and ourselves, creates a culture that can heal the wounds inflicted at the previous level. Individuals evolve much more quickly than societies can. So, very little structural change is seen until about ten percent of the population achieves this next level. After that the balance shifts and the new level dominates until its shadows, pitfalls and pathologies begin to emerge and further change becomes necessary.

I add, as an **Integral Spoiler**, the deep values learned at each level. Even though we only appreciate them when we get to level seven, once we have mastered the skills to cope with a particular life condition, we carry these values with us and can call upon them when the situation warrants. For nothing essential is lost as we evolve.

Basic Resources for Part Three

Aurobindo. *The Life Divine*. Pondicherry, India: Sri Aurobindo Ashram, 2010.

Beck, Don Edward and Christopher Cowan. *Spiral Dynamics: Mastering Values, Leadership and Change.* Malden, MA: Blackwell, 2005.

Corbett, Joe. "Social Transformation: Toward a More Just Kosmos." Integral World (http://www.integralworld.net/corbett1.html).

McIntosh, Steve. *Integral Consciousness: How the Integral World Is Transforming Politics, Culture and Spirituality.* St. Paul, MN: Paragon House, 2007

Wilber, Ken. *Integral Spirituality: A Startling New Role for Religion in the Modern and Postmodern World*. Boston: Integral Books, 2006.

_____. *A Sociable God: Toward a New Understanding of Religion.* Boston: Shambhala

Publications, 2005.

_____. *The Spectrum of Consciousness.* Wheaton, IL: Quest Books, 1977.

Part IV

WYSIWYG
[What You See Is What You Get]

The Stages as They Blossom[ed]

Religion Interpreted at the Different
Levels of Consciousness

10

In God's Image

And their memory made them extraordinary. In them, the unconscious knowledge of ancestral behavior called instinct had evolved. Stored in the back of their large brains were not just their own memories, but the memories of their forebears. They could recall knowledge learned by their ancestors and, under special circumstances, they could go a step beyond. They could recall their racial memory, their own evolution. And when they reached back far enough, they could merge that memory that was identical for all and join their minds, telepathically.

Jean M. Auel. The Clan of the Cave Bear

SurvivalSense [BEIGE]   [Instinctive / Reactive Values]
Evolution of Human Consciousness   *[Archaic]*

The third great "big bang" marks the evolution of consciousness. One branch of primates began to think. Early *homo sapiens* actually did very little real "thinking." They acted only slightly less instinctually than animals do. Gathered together in loosely tied bands, which gave them some advantage over other pre-human species, they survived. Aware of their vulnerability, the main focus of their lives was staying alive. Preliterate and barely conscious they lived off the land, relying on instinct and their heightened senses to satisfy their physiological needs.

Back in the Day: [As the Leading Edge] Human consciousness emerges around 100,000 BCE. The first human societies had no awareness of themselves as separate from nature.

Today: The Instinctive Self exists in infants and **.1 % of the adult population exercising 0 % of the power in the world.** It is found in starving masses, disoriented refugees, street people, the traumatized, and the senile.

Locus of Control: purely reactive to both internal and external states.

Worldview: urge / need to survive in the natural world as other animals do; but with a heightened sense of awareness. Values are reactive in character.

Basic Theme: Biological survival [reduce pain and avoid tension].
Motto: "Express self instinctively and automatically for biological survival."

What if He Comes Back?

It was dusk and the animals had come down to the water for a drink. Some of the early humans were among them. All of a sudden a lion leapt from the bushes looking for dinner. Without exception the animals, including the humans, scattered. After a while, the lion went away disappointed, looking for another opportunity for a meal. Slowly the animals returned to the water's edge and began to drink peacefully once again. But the early humans were still agitated. They were thinking. "What if the lion comes back?"

This is not about the lion. It is about the evolution of our brains. The hominid brain had tripled in size, peaking 500,000 years ago, when it became large enough to formulate ideas. Now that we could think, our thoughts terrified us. No other species worries. What if, is one of our most debilitating fears. Our imagination projects what might happen next, often envisioning the most desperate situation possible. Yet this apprehension, even though it is often groundless, can, and at times has, saved our lives.

The human condition is unique to us. No other species developed our powers of self-reflection and interpretation. As we came together and told stories of what had happened each day, we began to see patterns. We began to connect the dots. Certain behavior provoked certain responses. We began to see the relationship between cause and effect. If the lion did come back, we could be ready for it, if we had a plan. Together we could defend ourselves. The growing sense that there were spirits everywhere that could be appealed to for help strengthened our confidence in our own survival.

Shadow / Pitfalls / Pathology: barely human consciousness

Breakthrough: the awakening of a dependent self where being with others means safety and security. We reach a level of consciousness that shows that by joining together in stable family tribes we can establish conditions that bring greater prosperity to the group.

THE NEW BLOSSOM: THE PURPLE ᵛMEME

We can appeal to the spirits!

11

Say the Magic Words

In a world so empty of human life, there was comfort in the thought that an invisible realm of spirits was aware of their existence, cared about their actions, and perhaps directed their steps. Even a stern or inimical spirit who cared enough to demand certain actions of appeasement was better than the heartless disregard of a harsh and indifferent world, in which their lives were entirely in their own hands, with no one else to turn to in time of need, not even in their thoughts.

Jean M. Auel. The Plains of Passage

KinSpirits [PURPLE]   [Traditionalist Values]
                                   [Animism / Pantheism]

Back in the Day: [As the Leading Edge] Kin-Spirits emerged around 50,000 BCE. People joined together for greater safety. Tribal societies believed in curses, blood oaths, magical rituals, totems and taboos. Shamanistic prophecy and the wisdom of the elders provided security.

Today: The Magical Self - this worldview exists in children one to three years old, a time of profound innocence, and **10 % of the adult population exercising 1 % of the power in the world.** It is found in family rituals, is strong in Third World settings and neo-pagan religions, in belief in good luck charms, athletic teams, corporate "tribes."

Locus of Control: external, deferring to the more powerful or competent.

Worldview: close to nature. Looking through the lens of imagination, we see the world as magical and scary, full of mysterious powers that must be appeased. Following traditions creates order and ensures our existence.

Coping strategies: seek safety in the past. Obey the desires of the spirits and follow mystical signs, observe rites of passage and the seasons. Show allegiance to chief, elders, ancestors, and tribal customs.

Characteristic beliefs and actions: Now that we know that we know, fear and a sense of vulnerability dominate our consciousness. We remember past dangers and imagine the catastrophes that will occur if we do not follow the proper rituals.

Education: classical conditioning; direct training by elders.

Cognitive capacity: preconceptual / preoperational. Emotional thinking is very responsive to tribal pressure.

Basic Theme: keep the spirits happy and the tribe will be safe and warm.
Motto: "Sacrifice self to the ways of the elders and customs to ensure the safety of the group."

Technology: spoken language, foraging, fire, stone and bone tools.
Political situations: the village system - clan councils: kinship establishes bonds, suspicion of outsiders.
War: protect the ancestral traditions, rights of kinships and sacred places.
Economic traditions: resources shared by all, mutual reciprocity and barter.
Limits: where the spirits and our ancestors walk is sacred ground. The land beyond is evil, filled with hostile spirits and enemy tribes.

Values

Beauty: family allegiance.

Goodness: good of the spirits and of the tribe.

Truth: tribal stories, pronouncements of the leaders.

[**Justice:** banishment if taboos are broken, protection if one follows tribal traditions.]

Faith stage: Wonder-full, following the stories and legends of the tribe will keep us safe.

God: beings / spirits that control and affect nature. These forces must be appeased rather than angered.

> **Animism** everything possesses a spiritual essence.
>
> **Pantheism:** the universe is identical with divinity.

Prayer: magic incantations to persuade the spirits to Intervene on our behalf.

Morality: defend traditions, customs, and ancestral wisdom, protect our own kind.

Sin: if you don't follow the prescribed rules and rituals of the tribe, you will bring disaster on the tribe.

Religious Issues: Strong sense of enchantment, everything is alive; has soul [animism]:

Supersisto: "to stand in terror of the deity."

Natural Religion: rites, ceremonies -- >>> honor and influence the spirits.

The Myth of Nature

Humanity's first prayer was probably, "Help!" Life was harsh and short. They knew they were going to die, and when people did die, the survivors wondered where they had gone. The world was filled with spirits. The people thought that perhaps, when we die we go to join them. Early graves from this period show us that the people began to bury their dead with food and/or weapons beside them. This is our first indication that humans looked beyond this world to some sort of afterlife.

Nature was infused with mysterious forces that could/would protect or destroy at will. Sensing this spiritual dimension, the first humans asked, "Would we be safe if the spirits liked us? What do we have to do to get the spirits to protect us?" Their struggle to understand their relationships with the spirits began the process that eventually became known as "religion."

The drawings on the walls of Paleolithic caves of individual animals and groups of animals, some walking, some running, are breathtaking. Every image evokes emotion in the beholder. They teem with artistic naturalism. Whether they merely tell the story of the hunt or, as many believe, actually called to the spirits of the animals, inviting them to come and provide food for the tribe, they reflect a people very much in tune with nature. Interestingly, there are no depictions of war in the caves. We can, and we have easily dismissed these early ancestors calling them primitive, meaning backwards. In doing so, we have missed out on incredible insight, disconnected ourselves from nature, and lost a piece of our magical selves. These stories, these myths, are still there. They can help us reunite our consciousness to the tremendous and fascinating mystery of the universe.

Because humans could imagine how things happened, they had a better chance of survival. As they learned more about life, the next question was, "Where did the earth come from?" The earliest answer was from the animals. In different native traditions an animal enabled earth to exist. The Cherokee believed that Water Beetle dove down to the bottom of the water and brought back soft mud that spread out and became the earth. For the Iroquois, Muskrat succeeded in gathering dirt, which was placed on the back of a turtle. The tribes of the Pacific Northwest Coast honor Raven, who flew up and brought back the sun so there would be light. Spider Woman wove her web holding the universe together and taught the Navajo to create beauty in their own lives.

These creation myths spoke to the people's deep questions. They created a worldview, a framework for their lives together. While they are not literal, they continue to provide a suitable birth story, a history of sorts that binds the people together. Time is seen cyclically, the seasons follow one another. Rituals celebrate the changes in nature and life and connect then and now. The goal of life is to be connected. Paradise is living in harmony with nature where we will be safe and blessed.

Tribal stage churches are commonly referred to as cults, because of their focus on rituals. When Christians celebrate liturgy, they tap into these magical connections. It is here in common worship that all should be exposed to a true experience of the presence of God. If that does not happen, the actions can easily become mere movement and the human hunger for connection with the divine left unsatisfied.

Religion, as we have seen, is a collective response to "mystery." Religion connects us to God and to one another. By producing, revering and celebrating the myths that provided order and perspective to specific life conditions, humans found the meaning they so desperately needed. Gradually they came to know the gods. They connected with this Power, this Ultimate Meaning of Life, and they felt "safe." Then they told their stories. They gathered to celebrate the stories and passed them on to their children.

Darrell Fasching and Dell Dechant in their book *Comparative Religious Ethics* sketch how myth has adapted in different cultures. As life became more diversified and cities arose kinship ties were hard to maintain. How could life have meaning among strangers? The Myth of Nature transitions into the myths of the great world religions. Gradually, these alternate explanations of what it means to be human evolved. In China, the focus was the Myth of Harmony. All share the Tao in common. The Confucians found the hidden harmony of the universe and built their lives by going with the flow. India developed the Myth of Liberation. Each person is reincarnated over and over again until he or she realizes intimate connection with all that is. Then that person is freed from this worldly existence and finds true bliss.

The Middle Eastern people were less mystical in their approach. They saw the world linearly, it has a beginning, a middle, and an end. In the Myth of History, God, the creator, the All-powerful One who sustains and rules the world, will judge all at the end of time, rewarding the good and punishing the evil. Salvation is assured to those who believe and follow God's law.

In the interests of space, and because of general familiarity with the Western myth, the examples used will concentrate on Judaism, Christianity, and Islam. These religions of the "Book," share a belief in the same God and this God's relationship with three different people. Actually there are two books: The Bible and the Qur'an. The stories differ in detail only as we shall see.

NOTE: all religions, as the foundational meaning producing aspect of culture, can be experienced at all levels of consciousness. So, there are seven different ways to be Christian, Muslim, Jewish, Buddhist, etc.

Success generates the next problem: as the tribe becomes successful and relatively safe, the youth cannot understand the fears the elders continue to guard against. They become restless, yearn to break free of tribal rituals, now seen as holding them back. Allured by the freedom and power of the developing warrior culture, they desire to become free from tribal custom.

Shadow / Pitfalls/ Pathology: superstitions, omnipotent fantasy, animistic hallucinations, violent slavery to the group which opposes change or deviation.

Crack!!!

Breakthrough: the awakening of an egocentric self determined to break traditional ties and become powerful in and of itself

Breakdown: Purple sees the emerging warrior consciousness as a betrayal of kin loyalties.

Red looks back at the Magical Worldview as superstitious and naïve.

THE NEW BLOSSOM: THE RED ᵛMEME

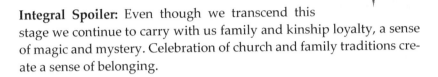

> Our Warrior God will protect us in battle,
> we must fight for what we believe in.

Integral Spoiler: Even though we transcend this stage we continue to carry with us family and kinship loyalty, a sense of magic and mystery. Celebration of church and family traditions create a sense of belonging.

12

Get Out of My Way!

We believe that cowardice is to blame for the world's injustices.

We believe that peace is hard-won, that sometimes it is necessary to fight for peace.

We believe in freedom from fear, in denying fear the power to influence our decisions.

We believe in ordinary acts of bravery, in the courage that drives one person to stand up for another.

We believe not just in bold words but in bold deeds to match them.

We do not believe in good manners. We do not believe that any of the virtue is more important than bravery.

Veronica Roth. Divergent *(The Dauntless Manifesto)*

PowerGods [RED]
[Egocentric]

[Exploitive Values]
[Polytheism / Henotheism]

Back in the Day: [As the Leading Edge]
PowerGods emerged around 10,000 years ago as tribes began to challenge one another for dominance. The impulsive ego began to reject tribal traditions. People followed strong leaders who took what they wanted without any concern for consequences.

Examples of this level are found in early Mythic Rome and Greece, Genghis Kahn, feudal kingdoms, epic heroes.

Today: The Impulsive Self - this worldview exists in children two to six years old and **20 % of the adult population exercising 5 % of the power in the world.** It is found in the "terrible twos," street gangs, ISIS, and those seeking status, power, and glory without concern for consequences or laws.

Locus of Control: internal, focused on personal power.

Worldview: very narrow outlook. The world is a jungle and only the strongest and most cunning survive by conquering others and taking what they want to fulfill their desire for power, status and glory. Raw power orders existence. Developing civilizations must go through this stage.

Coping strategies: Break free from any domination or constraint to please self as self desires. I call the shots without guilt or remorse. I take what I need using power and violence if necessary. I stand tall, expect attention, and demand respect without guilt or remorse.

Characteristic beliefs and actions: tired of tribal restrictions I must be what I am and do what I want no matter what the consequences. Violence is a way of life. I must avoid shame and get respect. I will be rewarded immediately for my conquests. Might makes right.

Education: Brutal expectations of young warriors, participation in conquest raids, admiration and imitation of warriors, listening to heroic sagas.

Cognitive capacity: preconventional, intuitive conceptual. Very assertive, can be aggressive.

Egocentric: true companionship in my group.

Basic Theme: Be what you are and do what you want, avoid shame, get respect right now.

Motto: "Express self [impulsively] for what self desires without guilt and avoid shame."

Technology: weaving, pottery, metal weapons.

Political situations: the empire system - empires ruthlessly controlled by the strongest

War: a way to extend fear and wield control, earn the right to rape and pillage.

Economic traditions: winner takes all, wealth distributed at the whim of the leader.

Limits: boundaries must always be enlarged, new lands and people are there to be conquered and ruled. Whatever we control is ours.

Values

> **Beauty:** victory, power, bravery.
> **Goodness:** pleasure, prestige, respect.
> **Truth:** our view of the world, our way of life.
> [**Justice:** the leader decides; might makes right.]

Faith stage: In-doctrination, one must conform rigidly to the rules to be considered faithful.

God: all-powerful, avenging, human-like [anthropomorphic] warrior, punishes those who fail.

Prayer: curse enemies, swear allegiance, do battle with evil.

Morality: respect, build reputation for passion and determination in a hard core world, there is no room for ambiguity.

Sin: to act shamefully, not to fight for the cause.

Religious Issues:

> Religious Violence in the name of God/the gods [Holy War]
> Militant, fundamentalist churches synagogues, and mosques
> Biblical and Qur'anic war stories and songs

The transition from foraging bands and tribes to empires and states precipitated more specialized and developed forms of religion. Organized religion emerged as a means of justifying a central authority that ruled as it saw fit. It created a bond controlling large numbers of unrelated people. Here we find the beginning of the shift from nature to history. Heroic myths, fantastic tales of human heroes and demi-gods stirred the passions and motivated the ego-driven impulses of the warrior consciousness.

The myths of the gods of Olympus, Rome and Babylon mirrored the passions of the aggressive, energetic, and powerful tribes that thirsted for domination and had little concern for others. Tying myth to history, paved the way for Western Civilization's greatest and most tragic moments. The gods were a family, each responsibly or irresponsibly controlling different areas of human life.

Polytheism, the belief in many gods gave way to henotheism, the belief that our God is the only one that matters. Finally the Hebrew people became monotheistic. They came to the conclusion that, Yahweh, their God was truly the only God. They denied the existence of any other gods. All other gods were considered false idols.

The Holy One that chose the Hebrews to be His people originated as a war god. Revealing His name and His plan to Moses, the Lord of Hosts [armies] led the slaves to freedom decimating the Egyptian gods and people in the process. This god was the best of all the gods [henotheism], and could and did lead His people in battle against all "others."

Battle was a religious experience. The warriors dedicated themselves to their god. All in the tribe were subject to the will of the gods and the commands of their chieftains. Just as our warriors fought with the enemy tribes, our god battled their god in the heavens. The winning god's people prevailed and the spoils belong to the god. The only way to give god his due was to slaughter the fallen enemy and burn all their possessions. Our god was honored as the smoke rose along with our prayers of thanksgiving into the heavens. The god received the choicest portions and the rest was divided among the people by the chief or chief priest.

Lawrence LeShan asks and answers the question, why humans love war in his 2002 book *The Psychology of War*. War, he tells us, makes us feel like we belong. We are fighting along with those we admire. We become important by adding our individual effort to the collective struggle for what is right. We are a part of the collective and yet still remain ourselves by adding our efforts to the cause. There is no guilt, only shame, the shame of not doing one's part to protect the holy cause.

War at the Red level is holy; there is no room for ambiguity, no sense of the individual self. "We" are on the correct path and everyone else is evil, because they reject the right, or stupid, because they're not smart or holy enough to realize that we are right. This exclusivism pervades the premodern world where already there is little recognition of the individual. Life is raw and rugged. There are no rules. There is no order. We fight because our way and/or our god's is threatened by the enemy's very existence. Sound familiar? This same poisonous ideology is alienating disaffected young people into becoming suicidal extremists today.

Today twenty percent of the world's adult population still holds this worldview. As we watch the terrible destruction in the Middle East and different areas of Africa we CANNOT forget the Western world's passage through this stage. The Crusades, called by the popes, wreaked havoc among Eastern Christians and Muslims alike in a misguided understanding that God willed that Latin Christians reclaim the holy city of Jerusalem. Europe was devastated by vicious fighting between Catholics and Protestants in the sixteenth century.

As the city states of Europe and the leaders of the churches realized the destructive power of this level of consciousness, they banded together and reestablished order and the violence subsided. Treaties were signed. The church began to speak of spiritual battles against evil. Warriors were disciplined. God would take care of these people in the afterlife, if not before. Vengeance belongs to God. The West may have outgrown crusade and jihad; but the hatred remained.

Success generates the next problem: egocentric values break down. We begin to see that in spite of all our efforts, life is beyond our control! Questions arise: What is life all about? Why was I born? Why can't I go on living? What happens when I die?

Shadow / Pitfalls/ Pathology: rooted in fear, ruthless, exploitation, anxiety, depression, phobias, excessive guilt, cannot build stable nations.

Breakthrough: the awakening of a purposeful self in search of the meaning of life and death. If life is a test, am I worthy of salvation? The violence becomes so great we need to search for the deeper meaning of life and death and find our answer in "God: the creator, designer, and ruler of this world,"

Crack!!!

Breakdown: Red looks back at the Magical Worldview as superstitious and naïve. And ahead at the Rule-based World as a loss of power, a surrender to weakness, compromising with evil, giving up the purity of our "cause."

Blue looks back at the Warrior Worldview as barbaric.

THE NEW BLOSSOM: THE BLUE ᵛMEME

If we sacrifice and obey the One True God we will be saved. This God will protect us.

Integral Spoiler: Even though we transcend this stage we continue to carry with us passion, energy, determination, courage, vitality, strength.

13

By the Book

Mother Culture whose voice has been in your ear since the day of your birth, has given you an explanation of how things came to be in this way. You know it well; everyone in your culture knows it well. But this explanation was not given to you all at once. Rather, you assembled this explanation like a mosaic: from a million bits of information presented you in various ways by others who share that explanation. You assembled it from the table talk of your parents, from cartoons you watched on television, from Sunday school lessons, from your textbooks and teachers, from news broadcasts, from movies, novels, sermons, plays, newspapers, and all the rest. This explanation of how things came to be this way is ambient in your culture. Everyone knows it and everyone accepted without question.

Daniel Quinn. Ishmael

TruthForce [BLUE]   [Sacrificial Values]
[Ethnocentric]   ***Beginning of Written History***   *[Monotheism]*

Back in the Day: [As the Leading Edge] TruthForce emerged around 3,000 BCE as tribes became religious nation-states created by and ruled by a Supreme Creator God. This level of consciousness dominated human thinking for thousands of years. Examples of this level are Hasidic Judaism, the Holy Roman Empire, Puritan America, codes of chivalry and honor, Confucian China, Fundamentalist Churches.

Today: The Rule/Role Self - this worldview exists in children seven to eight years old and **40% of the adult population exercising 30% of power in the world.** It is found in Boy and Girl Scouts troops, codes of honor, religious fundamentalists, the military, patriotic organizations.

Locus of Control: external, follow the will of authority.

Worldview: A violent and evil world is in need of law and order. This ordered existence is under the direct control of the One God, who is Ultimate Truth. Inequality is a fact of life. The focus is on the future. We must earn salvation and follow what is right.

Coping strategies: follow the given rules. Everything has been designed and is implemented by legitimate authority. Don't exceed your role. Conformity and humility will create discipline and will bring future happiness.

Characteristic beliefs and actions: Absolutist thinking, concrete-literal and fundamentalist belief. Life has meaning, direction, and purpose with predetermined outcomes and we must sacrifice ourselves to the Transcendent Cause, Truth, or Righteous Pathway, which is built on eternal, absolute principles. Follow the rules, do not challenge the authority of those delegated to speak for that authority. Impulsivity is controlled through guilt.

Education: Learn the rules and follow them explicitly. Have absolute trust in authority.

Cognitive capacity: Concrete operational. Concerned with procedures and routines.

Basic Theme: sacrifice earthly desires now in order to come to everlasting peace later. All should conform.

Motto: "Sacrifice self for reward to come through obedience to rightful authority in a purposeful way."

Technology: writing, law codes, agriculture, trade.

Political situations: the single-state system authoritarian centralized authority, hierarchical structures set by Divine intention, standing armies, doctrinal alliances.

War: protect our borders, preserve our way of life, "Evil" must be condemned and eliminated or it will contaminate the faithful, defend our "holy cause"

Economic traditions: earn rewards through hard work and discipline.

Limits: the world is ordered by and under the protection of the One true God who rules the entire world. God rules both this world and the next and will reward or punish us for eternity.

Values:

Beauty: everything approved by rightful authority that enhances the existing hierarchical structure; the certainty of knowing right from wrong.

Goodness: God's will, the law of God.

Truth: our sacred writings revealed to us by our God; They are to be taken literally.

[**Justice:** The Creator God makes the rules. You will be rewarded if you follow His will.]

Faith stage: Parade. Be quiet. Don't question. Keep marching.

God: The Warrior God of the Israelite people came to be seen as the most powerful God [Henotheism] and then the only God [Monotheism] who controls all things.

Prayer: Ask God in the right way for the right things to keep from being harmed. Worship and thank God so that you will be saved.

Morality: follow the rules exactly; Sacrifice self for God and others. Do your duty. Take responsibility or feel guilty.

Sin: defined by authority. Disobedience or non-conformity leads to punishment and disgrace.

Religious Issues: exclusive / inclusive

Good and Evil; [Saints and Sinners] final damnation or reward. [Hell presents a special problem.]

Exclusivism: belief that we're right and everyone else is evil.

Religious intolerance.

Evangelical and Fundamentalist fight for the American soul.

Conflicts within religions: Sunni – Shiite, Catholic – Protestant.

What is moral behavior?

In the Beginning . . .

To be in relationship is to share a story. The dominant Western understanding of God is based on the story of the God who saved the slaves and offered them a deal. The Hebrew people's experience in the desert formalized the covenant. In their story, the First Testament of the Bible, this all-powerful God would protect and defend His people as long as they followed the Commandments given to Moses. The God, who loves us, speaks and we obey! As the Hebrews conquered surrounding tribes and established a kingdom, they rejected all other Gods and became one God and one people in intimate relationship.

The Creator of the World had brought order to the chaos with a word. "God said" are the two most important words in the Bible. The words God spoke were so powerful that out of nothing came light and life. God continued to separate and shape the world as we know it for six days. God saw creation as good. On the sixth day, when God created human beings He saw them as **very** good. Then, on the seventh day God rested, and called all humanity to stop and marvel at creation and honor the Holy One, who does such wonderful things.

When God said, "Let us make humans in our image" to whom was God speaking? Was He speaking to the angels? To the animals? To Lady Wisdom, who was with God at creation? To the spirit? We may never know the answer; yet prayerful speculation has generated wonderful stories to inspire us. Perhaps the importance of the statement lies in the fact that from the beginning of time God is in relationship.

This story comes from the first chapter of the book of Genesis, the very beginning of the Bible. It sets the stage for all that follows. The point is that God is all-powerful! The second part of the myth, in the second chapter of Genesis, as we saw in chapter four, emphasizes God's love.

They fit together, yet the details differ. Like the story of the pig's house different stories were put together, because both were seen as important. One of the first decisions the followers of Jesus made was to keep this First Testament as part of their story. God's revelation to Muhammad includes the same basic story of creation but in a slightly different form.

The Myth of History has a beginning, as we have seen, a middle, as humanity leaves the Garden of Eden but not the relationship with God; and an end which will arrive when harmony is restored. We are living in the middle-time trying to overcome our "sinful" nature by following God's will as it is mediated by temple, church and mosque. This traditional understanding of religion, at this absolutist level of human consciousness, can be problematic because of the different interpretations of God's will between and within the great religions. The Jews see themselves as partners with God, **chosen** help fix this broken world [*tikkun olam.*] Christians follow the way of Jesus, the incarnation of God, who came to save us. Muslims believe the purpose of existence is to submit to God, Allah, in Arabic, and to accept Muhammad as his prophet.

An inherent obstacle in the myth of history lies in the fact that history is grounded in and carried by culture, which varies so greatly in different parts of the world. Even though, all at this traditional stage of religious beliefs agree that God must be obeyed, ancient enmities and current biases use religion to justify their ideologies. It is extremely difficult to separate cultural custom from religious law.

Traditional religion tames our impulses and curbs our passions. Interwoven with the Red passages of the scriptures are admonitions for peace. An eye for an eye might seem harsh today; but it was meant to prevent the escalation of violence common to the Warrior consciousness. There were rules, which gradually expanded to cover all areas of life. Following rules would bring salvation. God would punish those who broke them. There is no need for individual vengeance. Of course this only works when there is a certain amount of stability in the culture. When civilization slips back to the corruption, violence and deceit characteristic of Red consciousness, human consciousness regresses in the same manner.

The Middle . . .

The primary concern of people at this level of consciousness is to do good, avoid evil and be saved. We are called to sacrifice our will to God's now, so we will be saved for all eternity. As history progressed, the Roman Empire adopted Christianity as its official religion. This further blurred the boundaries and loyalty to government that was expected of the believer, because God had anointed the leaders of state as well as church. When the Roman Empire collapsed, the Church held unchallenged power until new political structures emerged. As barbarian tribes were conquered or converted, or conquered and forced to convert, a sense of order was established.

Christendom, this conglomerate of European city-states and kingdoms united by a common religion, was able to do much for civilization. Church law established what was right and what was wrong. Religion provided a certain sense of security and was able to demand civil peace as well. Centers of trade and learning flourished. Everyone knew what was expected of them. Though little consideration was given for the plight of the poor.

Power resided in the ones who knew God's will. The Pope, the leader of the Catholic Church, spoke to and for God. What was considered good or evil was determined by Church edict. The state was expected to enforce these decisions. The Church also held the keys to heaven; punishment for sin did not end with death. God became a distant judge. Fear of hell motivated most people to pray, to obey and to give money to the church in the hope that their sins would be forgiven. Salvation was not guaranteed by any means.

The mystery had been lost. A belief system replaced the relationship. All communication with the Almighty was brokered by the church. While many church leaders sincerely sought to do the will of God, others were more motivated by political ambition. Martin Luther challenged abusive church practices and rejected the need for papal interpretation of the will of God. His cry of "only faith, only scripture," and the church's refusal to dialogue with him, led to a spilt between the Catholics who remained loyal to the Pope and the Protestants who rejected papal authority. Neither side recovered the mystery; each developed and concretized different belief systems. Now there were several belief systems each claiming authenticity.

The End . . .

No, not the ultimate end, but the end, in the sense of the purpose of religion as it functions today. Christianity is practiced at the Traditional level by about seventy percent of those who claim membership. Some maintain membership more loosely; but follow God's will in order to be saved. They believe this One, True God still determines what happens in our lives and rewards and punishes appropriately. God can be influenced by prayer and sacrifice.

Evangelicals and Fundamentalists follow God's will as perfectly as possible. Most believe in the literal interpretation of the Bible. They have a personal relationship with God and actively promulgate their beliefs, expecting others to live as they do. Sin is primarily seen as offending God by disobeying His commandments as they are determined by the church. Jesus has redeemed us. His death on the cross has saved us from God's wrath.

Many Muslims have achieved this traditional level of consciousness. Like the Christians of the Middle Ages, their understanding of civil law is based on their interpretation of their scripture, the Qur'an. Their lives revolve around the worship of Allah, the Merciful. They pray five times a day, fast and give alms and if at all possible travel to their holy city, Mecca, at least once in their lifetimes.

Shadow / Pitfalls/ Pathology Rigid intolerance, micromanaging, archetypal role identification, fundamentalism, fascism.

Success generates the next problem: Unity creates a sense of earthly security and higher education. People begin to challenge traditional authority and test the possibilities of human reasoning. This leads to the realization that there are scientific explanations for what was thought to be God's will. The order created by distinguishing between good and evil in ever more minute categories is seen as oppressive. Authority continues to micromanage and does not recognize the integrity of individual decision-making. People become tired of conformity.

Breakthrough Transition: the awakening of a pragmatic self who challenges authority and tests possibilities, the individual self, capable of improving life conditions, emerges.

HUGE Crack!!!

Breakdown: Blue looks back at the Warrior Worldview as barbaric and senselessly destructive. Blue looks ahead at the Achiever Worldview as heretical and blasphemous and the Egalitarian Worldview as having lost its soul.

Orange looks back at the Traditional worldview as mindless and childish adherence to outdated rules.

THE NEW BLOSSOM: ORANGE ᵛMEME

God may have made the world; but we are able to improve it by means of science and human reason.

Integral Spoiler: Even though we transcend this stage we continue to carry with us a solid grounding in discipline, a sense of law and order, a strong sense of faith, and the ability to delay gratification. Blue can crack down on Red outbursts by appealing to Divine command. [Orange and Green cannot deal well with Red violence.]

Branding [Line / Level Fallacy]

There are many brands which have come to name the entire product. For example, Kleenex stands for all facial tissues, Clorox for bleaches and Xerox for copy machines. Ken Wilber warns of the danger of confusing one particular level of a line of consciousness with the entire line. It is here that a major fallacy occurs. One size can't fit all, which is the basic argument of this book. Most people confuse Blue religion with religion itself. The immediate, subconscious, picture we imagine when someone uses the word religion is the traditional, premodern understanding  of our relationship with God, at a Blue level of consciousness. Every level of consciousness has its own unique spiritual component. There are seven ways to be Catholic, or Muslim, or Jewish. And yet when believers and unbelievers alike think religion, this one Traditional level crowds out all other possible expressions of our relationship with Mystery.

For thousands of years the premodern concept of a world run by God was enough to inspire devotion and worship. It existed unchallenged as the fundamental source of meaning. Now as humans, especially in the West, have recognized the inadequacy of this view, traditional religion's image of God is too small. When Nietzsche claimed that God was dead, he was speaking of this Mythic God. The Holy One remains awesome mystery, beyond imagining; but the Traditional focus on belief in God's Theistic intervention and control no longer works. No, you are not sick because God wants you to be sick, you are sick because you didn't wash your hands and germs invaded your system.

Because Blue, Traditional religion has refused to accept the evolu-

---

** This fallacy also exists when we identify modern Newtonian science with scientific learning itself. When we think of science most imagine, materialistic experiments that can easily be proved. Scientific research, especially quantum science, has moved way past the provable and is probably one of the disciplines most comfortable with mystery.

 tion of humanity's spiritual/ religious imagination, we are stuck. Seventy percent of the world lives at this ethnocentric level or lower. Ideology and stagnant beliefs systems prevent new ideas from maturing. And it is the world's Great Religions who own the belief systems. Unless they are able to sanction new interpretations of the Great Myths, spiritual intelligence will not develop to keep pace with our intellectual, emotional, and moral intelligences. If our understanding of religion matches our level of consciousness, we continue to grow as a whole person. Ken Wilber uses the image of a conveyor belt or an escalator. A proper relationship with Mystery keeps us open to the new. Healthy religion and religion alone can enable this.

14

Buy the Book

We take off into the cosmos, ready for anything: for solitude, for hardship, for exhaustion, death. Modesty forbids us to say so, but there are times when we think pretty well of ourselves. And yet, if we examine it more closely, our enthusiasm turns out to be all a sham. We don't want to conquer the cosmos; we simply want to extend the boundaries of Earth to the frontiers of the cosmos.

Stanislaw Lem. Solaris

StriveDrive [ORANGE]   [Materialistic Values]
[Multiplistic]   *[Rationalism, Deism, Atheism]*

Back in the Day: [As the Leading Edge]
StriveDrive emerged in the 1700s and ushered in the "Modern" world. People began to recognize their own abilities and the inconsistencies and limitations of the "Premodern World." We realized we have the power to improve the world ourselves. Examples: The Enlightenment, democracy, the emerging middle class, evolution, corporate states.

Today: The Achiever Self - this worldview exists in children nine to fourteen years old **and in 30 % of the adult population exercising**

50 % of power in the world. Wall Street, Ayn Rand's *Atlas Shrugged*, cosmetic industry, multi-national corporations, scientific materialism, mainstream media are examples of this level of thinking.

Locus of Control: internal, focus on self-esteem and material success

Worldview: the world is a marketplace full of possibilities and opportunities. Truth is discovered not revealed. Optimistic, risk-taking, and self-reliant people will succeed. Societies prosper through strategy, technology, and competitiveness. We need to escape oppressive dogmatic systems.

Coping strategies: questioning, measuring, experimenting with the material universe, being optimistic, relying on self and other people to create and spread the abundant good life and increase material pleasures. Seek truth and meaning in individualistic terms.

Characteristic beliefs and actions: change and advancement are inherent within the scheme of things, progress is made by learning nature's secrets and seeking out the best solutions. Human ingenuity leads to knowledge which improves the human condition and creates prosperity. Competitiveness and risk-taking create a world-centered order. Success is measured in wealth and status.

Education: study under credentialed experts in separate disciplines, scientific experimentation, technical knowledge.

Cognitive capacity: formal operational, left-brain dominant. Strategic and future-focused.

Conventional

Basic Theme: Act in your own self-interest by playing the game to win.

Motto: "Express yourself [calculatedly] to reach goals and objectives without rousing the ire of important others."

Technology: scientific method, reason, logic, transportation and communication technologies, industrial revolution, medical miracles.

Political situations: the nation-state system multiparty democracy, treaties, diplomacy.

War: a commercial enterprise commenced on the basis of cost/benefit analysis, to advance our economic sphere.

Economic traditions: free-market capitalism, each acts on own behalf to prosper, success is measured by money, power and status

Limits: do business profitably within the next quarter.

Values

Beauty: knowledge, power and prestige.

Goodness: progress, liberty, material wealth, status, opportunity.

Truth: objective truth, reason, what can be seen and proved.

[**Justice:** impartial decisions based on the existing social contract.]

Faith stage: I've-got-to-be-me, I choose my path because it makes sense to me.

God: the Sacred ground of Being, not a physical reality. Theism, which believes in one God the creator of the universe, who intervenes in it and sustains a personal though distant relation to his creatures, is critically questioned. God may have made the world but does not intervene to help or punish. We have the skills to make things happen. [Deism]

Prayer: uplifting thoughts, meditation not petition.

Morality: there will always be losers. With confidence, ingenuity and hard work I can learn to set goals, to excel, to achieve material success.

Sin: oppression and social injustice, doing harm, not doing your best.

Religious Issues:

Skepticism, Agnosticism.

Separation of church & state.

Relationship between religion and politics

Deism, Humanism, Atheism

Secularism

Religion & modernity

Science vs. Religion

The Protestant Reformation was just the first crack in the premodern worldview. Scientific, political and economic revolutions followed. By the seventeenth century the effects of the emergence of a new worldview, the first in recorded history, were obvious. The Great Religions' mythic systems had been seriously challenged. Science and religion, like tectonic plates, crashed against one another causing psychic earthquakes throughout Europe. These clashes continue today.

For the first time history connected truth to actual fact, not just rhetoric. Only what could be seen and proved was true. Myth was ridiculed; and belief in God seriously questioned. Religion fought back claiming the literal truth of the Bible, labeling the skeptics as unbelievers and ended up marginalized. Science had finally reached its moment in time.

From the beginning science and religion have been at odds. The "new" Greek approach to thinking about nature was perhaps the greatest breakthrough ever made in human thought. That was in 600 BCE yet by Socrates' time other interests were considered more important. Earlier, in 3000 BCE, Egyptian scholars had invented their own form of writing and the sciences of mathematics, medicine and astronomy flourished. Yet this and all of the accumulated knowledge of the Western world remained subservient to religious myth. Human cognitive capacity was not widespread enough to support critical thinking.

During the ninth to eleventh centuries, Islam's Golden Age of Science, thriving centers of learning advanced our knowledge of science and mathematics and preserved many works of antiquity that might otherwise have been lost, by translating them into Arabic or Persian. The House of Wisdom in Baghdad was an unrivaled center for the study of the humanities. Its scholars accumulated a great collection of world knowledge, and built on it through their own discoveries.

The endeavor was supported by economic stability, religious unity and Qur'anic passages that place high value on education and emphasize the importance of knowledge. The holy prophet Muhammad is reported to have told his people to acquire knowledge even if they had to go to China. By the middle of the ninth century, the House of Wisdom was the largest repository of books in the world. It was destroyed in 1258 during the Mongol invasions. The invasions led to a breakdown in Arab cultural structure. This economical and intellectual regression cast doubts on the validity of human knowledge and learning centers became more focused on worship rather than study. Culture began to reemphasize absolute obedience and submission in all areas of life.

None of these early forays into the scientific realm ever achieved the critical mass necessary to affect the larger culture. Eventually it was in the West that the number of people who achieved Modern consciousness became large enough to overcome premodern thought's resistance. Cultural change requires more than abstract thought. Many circumstances contributed to the final breakthrough.

Just as the Arab Golden Age was ending, stability and order were reemerging in Europe. Universities were established, the first, the University of Bologna, was established in 1088. While charters issued by the Pope or the Emperor were required to ensure privileges, academic pursuit independent of civil and diocesan authority was protected. Earlier scientific discoveries were studied and enlarged upon; art, philosophy, and many other disciplines came into full flower during this Renaissance. This separation of culture and religion allowed investigation without fear of religious censorship. All of the energy stifled by the Church's insistence on orthodoxy was diverted into scientific investigation. What is this universe? How does it work? What can we do with it?

The Renaissance was the bridge between the Medieval and Modern Worlds. I want to emphasize the basic economic and political stability that must be present before human consciousness can embrace modernity. We're looking at a level of thinking that presupposes education. Freedom to think produces some sense of self-esteem and economic identity. [Don Beck estimates for a country today to transition to modernity people need to be earning about $3000 per capita, per year.]

Cultures cannot skip a developmental stage. Law and Order must precede Prosperity and Science. As the levels progress some of the earlier levels may by achieved more quickly; but if a stage is not completed regression seems inevitable. After the Dark Ages the West has maintained a political stability that enabled advancement to the Orange level of consciousness. Bitter wars were fought over what people believed; but not how they believed.

The Enlightenment was characterized by dramatic revolutions in science, philosophy, society and politics that ended the premodern world. Philosophers reexamined our understanding of the human consciousness and how this should affect political relationships. We set about learning the secrets of the universe from a fresh perspective. Critical thinking was born. Rene Descartes distinguished between mind and matter. He claimed that the objective world must be examined scientifically.

The most important insight of modernity is that the different disciplines are discrete, they stand separate from one another, they ask different questions and reveal different truths. For the first time science, art, spirituality, and morality were seen as different kinds of knowl-edge. This put the spiritual and the material in different categories, rescuing the material from its perceived inferior status. What could be seen could be proved, or disproved; truth was discoverable even if it was at the expense of "revealed" myth.

"Blue" religion could not accept this new scientific method that challenged its "truth." Consequently, it became antagonistic to the modern world and was in turn trivialized. Because religion was not, and chose not to be, included in modern conversation, Ken Wilber tells us, the four intelligences became three and a society was created that is inherently unstable. The spiritual line which asks and answers questions like, "What is it that is of ultimate concern? What is truly valuable?" was completely lost. The tragedy is that these are religious questions and cannot be answered adequately by any other discipline.

The differentiation between science and religion became dissocia-tive and many today, especially college students, Ken says, believe they must choose between the two. This seems to be the case because Blue and Orange, traditional religion and materialistic science are each dualistic systems. Each claims sovereignty and rejects the other's claim to truth. Orange has little room for spiritual intelligence and Blue has condemned modernity.

People at the Orange level of consciousness have dealt with this schism in different ways. Many have left organized religions and fol-low where their own spirituality and their private relationship with God lead them. The most extreme reaction rejects religion **and** its The-istic God outright. These self-proclaimed a-theists have established well-developed, exemplary value systems; they just don't include a God who created the universe or intervenes in human lives.

Deists are less radical in their approach. They recognize a Creator God who holds humans morally responsible for their actions. Because of humanity's reasoning capacity, this God has left the world in our hands to maintain and improve. God exists; but does not intervene for weal or woe. This partial rejection of religion sees the world as less supernatural and more practical. Thomas Jefferson ripped out all the Biblical passages pertaining to Divine miraculous behavior and was satisfied with the rest. Many of the founding fathers and mothers of the United States were Deist.

We see this in their insistence that church and state be kept sepa-rate. Religious practice was a personal right; but no religion was to be considered official. Our laws and customs, although influenced by personal religious sentiment, are determined by Social Contract. The idea that the United States is a Christian country is a recent and somewhat contrived notion that seeks to blur this distinction.

Separating church and state lead to another more subtle dilemma. How do we deal with the dichotomy of living two lives? The concept of sacred and profane is an idea that sociologist Émile Durkheim developed to illustrate the central characteristic of religion. Religion relates to the "sacred," that which is set apart; which leaves everything else secular or profane and subject to different values. By setting up special shrines to mark the areas where the One True God appeared, the faithful knew where God was. An unintended by-product of such designations leaves the rest of the world "unholy." One doesn't have to act the same way in the church parking lot as one does inside the church.

It is important to note that we do not develop at the same pace in every area of our life. Our different intelligences exist at different levels of consciousness. If however we continue to develop in all areas except the religious, a sort of spiritual schizophrenia begins to develop.

Ken Wilber argues that the best way to breach what he calls religion's steel ceiling is to recognize agnosticism as a valid spiritual intelligence. Agnosticism, a word coined in the nineteenth century, means that ultimate truth values concerning whether God exits or not cannot be known with absolute certainty. Isn't such questioning really an inevitable experience as human intelligence matures? If God is mystery, beyond human comprehension, by definition of the word, we cannot concretely prove or disprove God's existence. We can, however, know in a relational way that we are connected to something beyond our skin-encapsulated bodies and continue to allow our spiritual consciousness to evolve within or without organized religion.

Because we are cognitively able to reason abstractly we are able to find some truth in many different cultures' religious practices. We can experience the Divine Presence in many different ways. Orange consciousness moves past ethnocentric biases and is open, however tentatively, to new religious ideas. This worldcentric vantage point broadens our horizons and enables us to function more effectively in today's complex world. While this level of consciousness cannot integrate these differences, they can be and are tolerated.

Jenny Wade believes that we have a choice as we leave the Blue, absolutist world. We can move to the Strategic, Orange, level or move directly to the next stage, the Egalitarian, Green worldview. I am totally convinced that while this may be done, to skip this level radically stunts human growth. If we are to function as adults we must clearly and definitively claim our individuality. An adult takes responsibility for her or his own life, and develops the ability to articulate personal values and judge actions by personally chosen standards of behavior. To skip this step is merely to join a larger parade without the conscious thought that only comes from doing the hard work of self-examination. Many religious people have taken this route.

The image that many use for marriage, that the two become one, seems romantic; but it is really misleading. Which one do they become? Premodern patriarchical society pretty much answered that question. But today, in those places where expectations have grown, there are different possibilities. Relationship with God or another person in our complex, modernized world demands the presence of independent people. The two who marry remain two but create a third: their relationship.

If I as an adult self-defined person form any kind of relationship with another self-defined person there is no limit to the depths of joy, and frustration, we can both experience. The relationship works, or doesn't, but while it lasts it is the most exciting encounter possible, two fully human beings searching to be more. We become interdependent not codependent.

There is no foreseeable end to the consciousness levels we can achieve. Of course, human reason is only one of our intelligences. But it is the one that sets us apart. To refuse to do the work and establish my self as a self robs the world of a valuable gift and our relationships of genuine encounter.

Success generates the next problem: people become tired of competition. We recognize that life and nature are not so linear. There is more than what can be physically measured. What may be proved true is not the final truth. A sense of emptiness and lack of relationships develops.

Shadow / Pitfalls/ Pathology: loss of the spiritual dimension, materialism, greed, need to control the physical universe, unscrupulousness, identity crisis, role confusion, consumerism, ecological crisis...

Breakthrough: awakening of a sociocentric self striving for belonging and acceptance. Life becomes too materialistic and we strive for belonging and acceptance, inner spiritual harmony.

Crack!!!

Breakdown: Orange looks back at the Traditional Worldview as authoritarian and oppressive. And forward to the Egalitarian World view as humanity's most regrettable mistake: helping those who should be helping themselves.

Green looks back at Orange as greedy and materialistic.

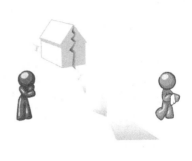

THE NEW BLOSSOM THE GREEN ᵛMEME:

God calls us to embrace and take care of one another, especially those who are marginalized. All people have dignity and must be treated with respect.

Integral Spoiler: Even though we transcend this stage we continue to carry with us meritocracy, excellence through competition, critical thinking.

In the Name of the Best Within Us

In 1991, a survey conducted for the Library of Congress indicated that Ayn Rand's book *Atlas Shrugged* was considered second only to the Bible as the book that made the most difference in people's lives. Ayn, a Russian émigré, vehemently opposed to socialism and religion, passionately summed up her philosophy in this 1957 novel about life in a dystopian United States in the very near future.

Atlas Shrugged debuted on *The New York Times* Bestseller List at number thirteen three days after its publication. It peaked at number three that same year, and was on the list for twenty-two consecutive weeks. It has continued to sell strongly; but sales increased following the 2007 financial crisis. *The Economist* reported that on January 13, 2009 the fifty-two year old novel ranked number thirty-three among Amazon's top-selling books. By April it ranked number one in the "Fiction and Literature" category at Amazon and number 15 in overall sales. Why is it so popular? What message could compel so many fiercely loyal readers and at the same time appall so many others?

The heroes in *Atlas Shrugged* all dramatize the novel's theme: The mind is humankind's tool of survival. Every advance that makes human life on earth possible is a product of the reasoning mind. Ayn Rand's philosophy, Objectivism, claims that the mind is the fundamental means by which a human person survives in stark contrast with the claims of the two dominant philosophical schools of modern western culture, Marxism and Christianity.

Is this a rational delusion or a magnificent expression of the human spirit? John Galt, the hero, lives by his own code. "I swear by my life and my love of it that I will never live for the sake of another [person] nor ask another [person] to live for mine." He rigidly adheres to this vow and asks all who follow him to live by it as well. Let this sink in. Read it again. Ask yourself if you could or should live by that standard. As Ayn explained during her interview with Mike Wallace in 1959, a person can choose to be open to love and friendship, to giving and receiving. But she adamantly reinforced her point; it is a **choice** based on what the person perceives as good for him- or herself, not an obligation imposed by society.

I believe we must make that declaration and live by it for a day, or a week, or for several years if necessary. To be an adult is not a matter of years gained but of a life claimed. When the lines were drawn more definitively and the consequences of such choices more threatening, as it is today in so many other countries, real courage is needed to stand by our beliefs. On the contrary in our perfectly correct Western world we defend everyone's right to free expression.

Yet how many of us do the real work necessary to stand as an individual claiming our "self" proud to be who we are? This step **cannot** be skipped. But neither can it be invoked in only one area of life. Ayn Rand has been called the "Goddess of the Marketplace" by those who apply her theory to unbridled capitalism; calling for absolutely no government interference in the stock market. Yet many of those same people advocate Blue, unbendable moral codes that ignore individual conscience and personal rights in our private lives.

Many of *Atlas Shrugged's* most ardent fans reject it as they grow older. This is consistent with the pattern we follow. As we move to the next level of consciousness, somehow we have to disparage where we've been, in order to justify where we're going. Contrary to popular political opinion, to change your mind because of new insights is an adult thing to do. No, this step cannot be skipped; but neither is it the last step. It also must be **transcended**. Nevertheless, we carry with us, wherever we go, the lessons learned from the books and stories that captured our hearts and changed our lives.

I believe that Ayn Rand expected each of us to be our best selves, whatever that means. Her heroes dominated the story; but anyone living to his or her potential was seen as heroic as well. We are not expected to measure ourselves by John Galt's or anyone else's standards. But we are expected to stand as self-defined adults. This level of maturity reflects Abraham Maslow's self-actualization stage; and is essential to further healthy development.

15

Bypass the Book

Faith and reason are dreams arising from the same wistful belief.

David Brin. Foundation's Triumph

HumanBond [GREEN]
[*Sociocentric*]

[Personalistic Values]
[*Spirituality, Ecumenism, Relativism*]

Back in the Day: [As the Leading Edge]
HumanBond began in the 1850s as people began to sense the dignity of the human person and the inherent oppression in both the Blue and Orange Worldviews. Sensitivity toward the minority, the marginalized and the environment developed. Examples: ecological sensitivity, postmodernism, socialistic health care, humanistic psychology, political correctness, and diversity movements, human rights movements,

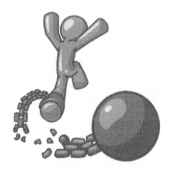

Today: The Sensitive Self - this worldview exists in young adults sixteen to twenty-one years old **and 10 % of the adult population exercising 15 % of power in the world.** It is found in communes, The World Council of Churches, the Parliament of the Worlds' Religions, the ACLU, Ben & Jerry's, sensitivity training, Doctors without Borders, Greenpeace.

Locus of Control: external, focus on aligning with like-minded peers.

Worldview: the world is a place where, freed from dogma and greed, we share life with all creation. It is anti-hierarchal and feelings supersede rationality. Spirituality and human development are seen as very important.

Coping strategies: break loose from biased, prejudiced expectations. Seek to embrace and understand all people, especially those who have been rejected by society. All people and their ideas must be respected.

Characteristic beliefs and actions: spread the Earth's resources and opportunities equally among all. Reach decisions through sensitivity, caring, reconciliation and the consensus process. Authority is now vested in the group. Appreciate the diverse views of all beliefs and cultures.

Education: no longer the realm of scholars, each viewpoint must be given equal status.

Cognitive capacity: early vision logic, right brain dominant. People are the highest value.

Basic Theme: seek peace within the inner self, explore dimensions of caring communities, appreciate diverse views, listen well, go for consensus, emphasize group needs.

Motto: "Sacrifice self-interest now in order to gain acceptance and group harmony."

Technology: non-violent resistance to injustice, deconstruction of the icons of Western Culture, naturopathic medicine.

Political situations: the planetary system social democracies, self-directed teams, shared leadership, International Court of Justice.

War: only if necessary to punish those who commit "crimes against humanity" and protect the victims.

Economic traditions: universal education and health care. All should benefit equally.

Limits: the environment, all should be open to all.

Values

>**Beauty:** nature, the imperfect.
>**Goodness:** sustainability. Whatever is best for all people and the planet.
>**Truth:** subjective. Whatever is true for you.
>[**Justice:** all people must be treated equally, the poor and the marginalized must be welcomed.]

Faith stage: You-could-be-right-too, tension and ambiguity are acceptable.

God: Love, Energy, Creative Intelligence. All worship same Mystery in different ways.
Prayer: Eastern spiritual practices, we send and receive healing energy.
Morality: practice acceptance, healing and justice.
Sin: alienation, bias, indifference.

Religious Issues:

> The Social Gospel
> Catholic Social Teaching
> Human rights
> Ecumenism
> Relativism
> SBNR / The Nones
> Rediscovery of spirituality
> Ancient and new wisdom traditions
> Competition between traditional and postmodern spirituality for the soul of modernity

In the middle of the nineteenth century the focus shifted again. The postmodern world began to emerge and it rejected both Blue Dogmatism and Orange Materialism. Postmodernism is a much-debated term often applied to different academic fields; but, in essence, it is a reaction to the modern idea that objective science can explain reality. Actually it questions the foundation of all past knowledge, including mythic religion.

The egalitarian worldview despises any kind of hierarchy that says anything is better than anything else. It goes so far as to assert that there are no universal truth claims. Decision-making moves from facts and logic to feelings and personal experience. Truly pluralistic, this altitude can see things from many perspectives and embrace a more inclusive compassion that thinks, feels, and acts globally. We are now able to move beyond the mere tolerance of the modern level to embracing and honoring the other. All ideas, all religious traditions are seen as equally valid.

People were not looking for new answers to old questions. They were asking completely different questions. Patriarchy, hierarchy of any kind was no longer seen as the way things have to be. Religious hierarchy was seen as especially oppressive. New opportunities exposed the richest most successful nations to exciting unorthodox ideas. Different religious experiences from the East opened up new ways to grapple with the ambiguities of life.

The modern world was wrong; we cannot live without a sense of transcendence. Religion resurfaced but in different forms. Spiritual exploration of all kinds was encouraged. We began to see commonalities among the religions of the world, not just differences. At the center of the great religions the similarity is extraordinary. Oneness is the core teaching of Judaism which calls its adherents to inclusive solidarity with the needy. Jesus interpreted our relationship with God and others as loving unconditionally. All but one of the one hundred fourteen suras of the Qur'an begin with, In the name of God, boundlessly compassionate, infinitely merciful.

The Protestant Social Gospel and Catholic Social Teaching began to raise specific issues calling for justice for the poor. Dogma and greed were seen as oppressive forces that have brought untold suffering to the marginalized. All people must be treated with dignity; slavery of every kind must be eliminated. Physical slavery was challenged and outlawed. Mental and spiritual slavery continue to be condemned. To be in slavery is to be at the mercy of arbitrary power; the fewer choices people have the more they are enslaved. The often hidden evil of slavery lies in the persistent insecurity it fosters. All should truly be equal.

In the name of equality even natural hierarchies are rejected. While in its emergence phase this was a welcome relief, as Green consciousness has become more widely accepted in the West, many are beginning to experience its shadow side. History is seen as merely fictional interpretations. There are no facts only opinions. We create our own reality. It is here that those who have not achieved adult consciousness are lost. With no clear direction, no process for personal decision-making, they follow those who appeal to their sense of good, and lash out, often viciously, at their opponents, without understanding the complexity of the situation. Postmodernists accept so much diversity that they can't create any unity. We have lost our center.

The predicted end of organized religion did not occur, though many mainline religions lost a significant number of members, particularly among the young. The numbers of people who claim no religious affiliation steadily rises. This mass exodus has devastated European Christianity and is growing in the United States. Called "SBNR," spiritual but not religious or just "the Nones," one third of this group claims to be atheistic or agnostic.

Traditional religion sees authority and God as something external; while the postmoderns think more about God in terms of spirit existing everywhere and within everyone. They see their own experience as authoritative and need no other approval. Their spirituality may be expressed by ecological awareness, political correctness, diversity movements, universal human rights, multiculturalism, humanistic psychology, liberation theology, or the human potential movement.

Freedom to follow one's own path has enabled all of the previously repressed expressions of religion to resurface. God is invoked from the Warrior consciousness of ISIS, religious claims are made in the name of the Cosmic Christ, and TV evangelists vie with policy wonks for Sunday morning TV viewership. One of the reasons that the culture wars are so vicious is that they are fueled by many different levels of religious sentiment. All must be accepted but we haven't yet achieved the consciousness to deal with the animosity that accompanies the diversity.

Many others are opting for a post-Christian interpretation where nothing rises higher than anything else. There sometimes seems to be an uncritical acceptance of all values and practices. Yet, for all their inclusiveness, they are often angry at the tribal, warrior, traditional, and modern church. The division between Traditional and Postmodern churches is so great that it virtually produces two different religions both using the same Bible and the same language. Fundamentalists and extremists in all religions claim credibility. With no central authority acknowledged, who can judge a particular behavior to be outside the acceptable norms of any religion? By embracing the narcissism and the message of "prosperity" postmodern religion can easily turn into spirituality in the service of the ego.

Marcus Borg and Bishop John Shelby Spong and some Catholic

theologians are trying to articulate a postmodern Christian position by focusing on a non-theistic relationship with God that is transforming; a relationship that can and will change your life. God is the non-material layer or level or dimension of reality all around us. God is more than the universe, yet the universe is in God. This is called panentheism. God is not somewhere out there; but right here evolving with the universe. "In him we live and move and have our being." [Acts 17:28]

The Pew Research Center Study found that the percentage of American adults who describe themselves as Christians has dropped by nearly eight percentage points in just seven years to 70.6% in 2014. Over the same period, the percentage of Americans who are religiously unaffiliated , describing themselves as atheist, agnostic or "nothing in particular," has jumped more than six points to 22.8%. The share of Americans who identify with non-Christian faiths has risen to 5.9%. Growth has been especially great among Muslims and Hindus, although from a very low base.

Religious "nones" now constitute 19% of the adult population in the South, 22% of the population in the Midwest, 25% of the population in the Northeast and 28% of the population in the West. The full report is available on the website of the Pew Research Center's Religion & Public Life project.

Success generates the next problem: as more rules and customs are relativized there is no longer a recognized standard of acceptable behavior; life becomes ambiguous. We get so wrapped up in collective decision-making that nothing gets done. We become more aware of the costs of entitlements. We begin to yearn for solutions.

Shadow / Pitfalls/ Pathology: committeeism, inauthenticity, deadening and excessive relativism, lack of discernment, interminable attempts at consensus, the 25 to 1 tie vote, refusal to make value judgments, contempt for modernism and traditionalism. If everyone gets a trophy, what happens to its value?

Breakthrough: the awakening of an interdependent self not needing approval but able to collaborate. We become more integrated by acknowledging and reawakening the essential values of every previous worldview. This level is willing to take responsibility for the health of the whole spiral.

HUGE WORLD-THREATENING CRACK!!!

Culture War

The most obvious danger today are the religious culture wars that fuel the violence in the Middle East and incapacitate political decision-making in the United States. Traditional, Modern and Egalitarian consciousnesses vie with one another for moral authority. **People of good will are embroiled in battle to protect their sense of God.** This is an extremely important point to note, each of these consciousnesses **believes it is right** and the others wrong, and is incapable of seeing any good in the any other position.

Breakdown: Green looks back at the Traditional and the Modern Worldview as authoritarian and oppressive. And forward to the Integral Worldview as compromising principle. Green refuses to make any hierarchical decisions. It's all or failure.

Yellow, integral consciousness is the first to appreciate all levels of consciousness.

THE NEW BLOSSOM THE YELLOW ᵛMEME:

God is all-encompassing love, the power of creative intelligence and evolutionary impulse.

Integral Spoiler: Even though we transcend this stage we continue to carry with us a sense of human rights, recognition of human potential, compassion and inclusion, renewed spiritual freedom and creativity

Bratty or Brilliant?

E galitarian consciousness should have taken the edge off the religion-science conflict; but it didn't. An inherent flaw in postmodernism, that Ken Wilber labels the **Pre/Trans Fallacy**, can actually make is worse.

Three stages summarize the growth of human cognition. Pre-rational or Pre-conventional, the level before a person is capable of making true moral decisions, Rational or Conventional, when a person achieves the ability to follow rules and keep agreements made, and Trans-rational or Post-conventional when a person's conscience develops to the point that he or she is capable of acting beyond law or custom in response to a complex situation.

According to Ken Wilber, because they are not at the rational or conventional stage of consciousness, the pre-rational and trans-rational stages can be easily confused. Wilber realized that people can either dismiss calls to greater consciousness by reducing trans-rational spiritual realization to pre-rational regression, or reward immature behavior by elevating pre-rational states to the trans-rational domain.

In other words, when someone acts differently how can we know if they're being a brat or offering a brilliant, although unusual, solution?

The Egalitarian consciousness is particularly vulnerable to this fallacy when it labels all who are at the margins of society as victims or when it treats the rantings of adults acting like eight year-olds with the respect due the insights of a mature human being. Often what is needed is empowerment not enabling. Careful discrimination is necessary in order to recognize and support the brilliant and contain and challenge the brat. Many at the Egalitarian level are incapable of such discernment. It is only at the next, Integral, level that this skill will be developed.

Part V

ANFSCD
[And Now for Something
Completely Different]

...The Momentous Leap We Have Been Waiting For...

Integral Consciousness

If there is one thing these previous stages all have in common, it's the belief that their stage represents the "correct" way of behaving and the only way of seeing the world correctly. They are all dualistic: we're right and all the others are completely or mostly wrong. We can see this playing itself out every day in our

culture as the religious fundamentalists, the rational materialists, and the pluralistic postmodernists all continue to insist that their values are the only "true" values, and everyone else's values are either delusional or outright demonic. While it might sell newspapers, the real question is whether we will survive this dissonance? Have we gone too far down the road of hatred and violence to recover our sense of balance?

We stand disconnected as the earliest humans were, seeking a way to survive. What is it that *homo sapiens*? What is it that we know? Will we breakthrough to this next level, or will we blow each other up? The word Armageddon is on too many lips to be sure that we will survive.

Radical Shift: Second Tier Consciousness

Integral Consciousness can appreciate all the different worldviews and understand the seemingly contradictory behavior of the First Tier levels of consciousness. It emerges in the face of much resistance from first-tier thinking especially Green which will not prioritize anything.

It operates out of the same energy as the First-tier BUT in nondual ways. Its PRIME DIRECTIVE: to work for the health of ALL THE ^VMEMES!!!

In *A Theory of Everything*, Ken Wilber shows how the different first-tier memes resist the emergence of Integral Consciousness. Scientific rationalism (Orange) can't accept the integration of the spiritual with the material. Fundamentalism (Blue) is still outraged at not being the acknowledged authority. Extremists (Red) ignore every attempt at order altogether. Integral consciousness is way beyond Magic's (Purple) comprehension. Green accuses second-tier consciousness of being oppressive because it makes choices.

The first-tier levels fixate on the pathologies of the other worldviews and refuse to acknowledge any of their strengths. Integral Consciousness operating in a non-dual manner recognizes both and accepts people at each level where they're at. Yellow's primary goal is not to expect people to change levels; but to help them recognize and develop the healthy aspects of their level. What's more, if people are able to see that others appreciate their gifts, they are much more open to thinking about taking the next step in their own development.

16

What's Your Point?

This is your last chance. After this, there is no turning back. You take the blue pill—the story ends, you wake up in your bed and believe whatever you want to believe. You take the red pill—you stay in Wonderland, and I show you how deep the rabbit hole goes. Remember: all I'm offering is the truth. Nothing more.

Morpheus. The Matrix

FlexFlow [YELLOW]   [Existential Values]
[Systemic]   **Parallels BEIGE - focus: survival**   **[Panentheism]**

Today, as the Leading Edge: Flex-Flow emerged in 1950. A few people began to see the larger picture. Clare Graves and others began to grasp this next jump in consciousness. They could now work with the entire spectrum of inner and outer human development. At this radically new level of understanding, the best principles of each of the lower levels of consciousness can be embraced 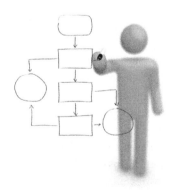 and accepted. Having a firm grasp on reality they are able to activate the gifts appropriate to the level of the situation. Examples of Integral thinking are Carl Sagan's astronomy, Spiral Dynamics, systems thinking, "Third Way" politics, chaos theory, Whole Foods, Southwest Airlines.

The Integral Self - this worldview exists in **5% of the adult population exercising 5% of power in the world.** Examples: Ken Wilber, Clare Graves, Don Beck, Steve McIntosh

Locus of Control: internal, focus on personal growth and learning.

Worldview: the world is a complex organism of natural hierarchies and systems forged by differences and change. Knowledge and competency should supersede power, status, and group sensitivity. I must recognize the legitimacy and evolutionary necessity of all previous stages without letting any one level of consciousness dominate.

Coping strategies: flexibility, spontaneity, and functionality create order. I must awaken the maximum number of streams of evolution possible. I insist on achieving results by using the strengths of all previous levels. Distinctions are made in order to clarify our perception. There are rules; but they are flexible.

Characteristic beliefs and actions:
Differences can be integrated into interdependent natural flows. The most serious problem today is the survival of the planet. I must recognize the magnificence of existence and see that it continues. I am responsible for the overall health of the Spiral and yearn for large-scale social awakening. All knowledge must be placed in the context of the natural hierarchies of the universe to create and implement the best possible solutions. I need to be flexible enough to change plans as needed: to adapt, blend, mesh, as I access and gather new information.

Education: becomes self-directed, open to learning at anytime from any source.

Cognitive capacity: late vision logic [integration of both the right and left brains] first level to be able to comprehend the complexity of the issues we face in creating a sustainable society.

Basic Theme: integral synthesis. Live fully and responsibly as what you are and learn to become. Strategize to help all [most] win. Self-connect to systems and others carefully.

Motto: "Express self so that all others, all beings can continue to exist."

Technology: computers/digital technology, quantum science.

Political situations: supranational governance, stratified democracy, using the best possible evidence to benefit as many as possible. Will make new decisions tomorrow to include more.

War: some conflict between the levels is inherent and inevitable. As a world we have only recently moved past violence as a solution to solving our problems.

Economic traditions: global systems economy; share with competent and knowledgeable at any level.

Limits: expanding but real orientation toward sustainability.

Values
>   **Beauty:** nature and the arts of each level, unification of extreme contrasts.
>
>   **Goodness:** evolution, attending to the health of the Spiral.
>
>   **Truth:** is not absolute. Fact and meaning must be taken into consideration. Values evolve, truth continues to be uncovered.
>
>   [**Justice:** create a system where the most possible good can be done to the greatest number of people. Systems must change constantly as we learn more ways to improve them.]

Faith stage: Compassionate Connection, All is one.

God: immanent and transcendent, all-encompassing love, the power of creative intelligence and evolutionary impulse.

Prayer: healing, helping inspired states of consciousness. Intimate experience of God.

Morality: individualized beliefs and behavior is right and proper if it is based on today's best possible evidence. What was right yesterday may not be right today.

Sin: failure to see larger picture. Remaining in dualism.

Religious Issues:
   Harmonizing science and religion
   Compassion for all worldviews
   Faith more important than religion
   God and evolution

According to Clare Graves theory, the Second Tier functions like the next octave in musical notation, the same sound only higher. He predicted that the same eight issues would reappear as our consciousnesses evolved. In the initial chaos of Beige there was no clear direction. This certainly parallels our experience today. While many have very clear ideas about where we should go and what we should do, there is no central agreement. Many wonder about the survival of our planet and our species. Where do we begin to integrate such diversity? Graves suggested that we, "Recognize, truly notice what life is and you shall know how to behave."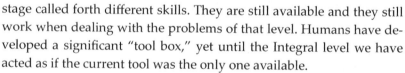

The first step is to reclaim what we rejected along the way. Go back and reclaim the gifts of all the previous levels. This is what the Integral Spoiler held onto at the end of each level of consciousness. Each stage called forth different skills. They are still available and they still work when dealing with the problems of that level. Humans have developed a significant "tool box," yet until the Integral level we have acted as if the current tool was the only one available.

Now we can work with existent reality. We, the ones who know that we know, have come to understand that there are many things that we don't know. We do, however, have a considerable understanding of our situation. We understand its complexity; but unlike the Egalitarians, Integralists are able to decide to do something. It may not solve the issue completely; but it does begin the process and all are patient with the fact that each step builds on the former. Behavior is right if it is based on today's best possible evidence. We will never have enough evidence to be "sure." We now realize there is no shame in changing course as we learn more.

Unlike the original humans we are not starting from scratch. But before we can gather in "tribes' as they did, we must disempower the extremists. The idea is not to get involved with criticism or controlling behavior. When we accept human nature as it is, yet stand firm in truth, basic human fears are assuaged. This is neither simple nor easy; but survival is at stake. The passion of the extremist's belief can be honored, while at the same time their destructive behavior is being censured and diverted or contained.

These steps lead to a new understanding of religion, a new bonding with Ultimate Mystery and each other. Integralists value all human appetites, we can function at all the levels of consciousness without being slave to any one of them. Spontaneity, simplicity and an ethics that makes sense for this particular moment in this particular situation move us in the right direction. We have learned that there is no one solution that will work in all places or at all times. With a certain sense of detachment, we realize that objective solutions must give way to communal undertakings. Faith in each other becomes more important than organized religion. Gandhi said, "Be the change you want to see in the world." That's certainly a wonderful concept, but the integralists have added, "What if the change that **we** want to see in the world is not good for the world?"

One of the greatest contributions integral consciousness is making to the world is the reclamation of spirituality. To many today, religion seems to belong mostly to the zealots, the fanatics, or the simpleminded, and to the detriment of us all it is still largely dismissed by the modern rational world. But spirituality is not the *product* of superstition, magic, and mythology, it just simply has not been allowed to evolve beyond superstitious, magical, and mythological interpretations. Remember the Line/Level Fallacy. Both Blue's religious fear of losing a sense of reverence and respect and Orange's skeptical scientific reductionism have prevented the emergence of higher levels along the spiritual line.

Spirituality has not been given an opportunity to shift from rigid belief statements to direct experience and discover its true voice in the rational and postmodern world. We were a bit too eager to eliminate the dogma, the myths, and the "us vs. them" ethnocentricity, and as a result have thrown the baby out with the bathwater. Luckily, integral spirituality rescues the baby. Not only does an integral approach to spirituality offer a way to evolve within each of the major spiritual traditions, (e.g. Integral Christianity, Integral Buddhism, Integral Judaism, Integral Islam, etc.), it also fosters the most inspiring and fruitful *interfaith* dialogues we have ever seen.

We are beginning to rediscover how the experiences of awakening, enlightenment, and atonement have been interpreted from person to person, culture to culture, all across the ages. Many are now reclaiming these experiences as a means of becoming whole and holy. These are without a doubt the most intelligent and insightful discussions of spirituality and science you will find anywhere on the planet. It is too early for noticeable structural change but as Pope Francis seems to know, the first reform must be attitudinal. Love, truth, and mercy form a container where new perspectives can be formulated.

By integrating the wisdom traditions of the great religions and philosophies of the world, we touch our deepest being and find there the connections we lost through past narrow-mindedness. This stage is very difficult for political or spiritual organizing to imagine structurally; but to the extent that we are able to connect through the virtue of compassion, we can relate intellectually, emotionally, morally and spiritually to reconstruct human relationships.

There have been five major catastrophes that have decimated life on this planet. Many believe we are headed for the sixth. We will either experience this catastrophic downsizing or balance the different levels of consciousness in some form of global consensus. This consensus will emerge only when a critical mass of people capable of moving beyond our current dualistic prejudices has been achieved. The integral estimation that about ten percent of the population at this level is needed before significant change is apparent. Currently the world hovers at about five percent of the adult population at this level.

Shadow / Pitfalls / Pathology elitist, insensitive, lack of patience with incompetence, works outside the group, seems insincere.

Systemic Problems haven't emerged yet as there are so few systems, structures at this level.

Yet a new Breakthrough is already occurring: the awakening of experiential self using integral knowledge to restore natural harmony, and balance.

THE NEW BLOSSOM THE TURQUOISE ᵛMEME:

We find the divine in the human heart. Namaste.

 The Fully Integrated Person with the best parts of all the previous levels embraced begins to see global connections.

17

Connected!

Dr. Grace Augustine: [to Selfridge] Those trees were sacred to the Omaticaya in a way you can't imagine. I'm not talking about pagan voodoo here. I'm talking about something REAL and measurable in the biology of the forest. What we think we know is that there's some kind of electrochemical communication between the roots of the trees. Like the synapses between neurons. Each tree has ten to the fourth connections to the trees around it, and there are ten to the twelfth trees on Pandora...That's more connections than the human brain. You get it? It's a network, a global network. And the Na'vi can access it. They can upload and download data and memories at sites like the one you just destroyed.

James Cameron. Avatar

WholeView [TURQUOISE]   [Holistic values]
[Cosmopolitan]   Parallels PURPLE - focus: connections   [Mysticism]

Today, As the Leading Edge: WholeView emerged in the 1970s. It operates by holonic thinking, which views the world as a single, dynamic organism with its own collective mind. It sees human beings as both distinct from and a blended part of a larger, compassionate whole. Examples include: Ken Wilber's work, Teilhard de Chardin, James Lovelock's Gaia Theory.

The Holistic Self: this worldview exists in **.1 % of the adult popula-**

tion exercising 1 % of power in the world. Examples: Steve Mcintosh, Pope Francis, the Dalai Lama, Orson Scott Card, Jesus, Muhammad, mystics.

Locus of Control: external, focus on connecting with the Transcendent.

Worldview: the world is an elegantly balanced system of interlocking forces. We see the synergy of all life. Multi-tiered consciousness. Renewed spirituality and a willingness to sacrifice for the whole.

Coping strategies: Compassion, Oneness, See the world as a global community [Tribe.] Reverence the wisdom of the "elders."

Characteristic beliefs and actions: energy and information permeate the Earth's total environment. Holistic, intuitive thinking and cooperative actions are to be expected; ecological interdependency.

Education: learn from every experience of connectedness, blends feelings and technology.

Cognitive capacity: early psychic.

Basic Theme: we experience the wholeness of existence through mind and spirit. We see the connections that exist among all creation.

Motto: "Experience the wholeness of existence through mind and spirit."

Technology: Quantum physics, high tech and high touch, social media.

Political situations: holonic democracies, Whole-Earth networks, macro-solutions.

Economic traditions: resources and learning distributed by need, not want, so all can survive with enough.

Limits: multiple levels woven into one conscious system not based on external rules or group bonds.

Values out beyond right and wrong

Beauty: mystical forces that permeate all existence.

Goodness: compassion.
Truth: ecological alignment, everything connects to everything.
[**Justice:** transformative. Works to repair relationships.]

Faith stage: Mystical Connection

God: Oneness; the Three Faces of God.
Prayer: the direct mystical experience of Oneness.
Morality: love, competency, compassion.
Sin: seeing self as separate.

Religious Issues:
   Finding connections with the divine self and all of creation
   The Three Faces of God
   The Cosmic Christ
   The Mysterious Universe
   Gaia Theory

Yellow Integral consciousness has not had time to develop structurally at all and yet WholeView Consciousness is already emerging. Perhaps they are meant to work together. Turquoise is the second-tier parallel to Purple. Magic meets mysticism. The only difference is that Purple level saw humanity in jeopardy at the hands of magical forces, while Turquoise thinking sees this delicately balanced system of forces in jeopardy at humanity's hands. Both see and yearn to connect with Mystery.

In the movie Avatar, Selfridge dismissively calls the natives "blue monkeys," a throwback to modern society's disdain for lower forms of life. The point of the movie is that the Na'vi people have evolved to a point where they have connected with the physical energy of the planet, at what would be considered the Turquoise level. The planet is alive and they are intimately connected with it and this has scientific value. Of course, the modern world is missing this point completely.

From the first-tier perspective it is difficult to distinguish between pre-rational magical and post-rational mystical behavior. Since they are both nonrational they can easily be confused. This is an example of the Pre/Trans Fallacy. The magical can be elevated to the mystical stage as when early tribal societies are romantically seen as shining examples of advanced stages of spiritual growth. At the same time, the truly mystical experiences of both religion and science can be dismissed as mere superstition.

Mystical consciousness which sees the self as part of a larger, conscious whole is no longer reserved to a rarified few. Today all are called to be mystics: to experience directly the presence of the Divine. We no longer need religious and/or spiritual experiences to be mediated by priest, rabbi or imam. Union with the Absolute, the Infinite, "God" is seen as the aim of Turquoise spirituality.

Great leaders are often way ahead of their time; leaving their followers to interpret their message as best they can; even though the followers are limited by lower levels of consciousness. Fortunately, the leader's teachings remain to guide and inspire deeper insights as their followers become ready to appreciate them. Today, Christians can find new meaning in Jesus' words about his being "one with the Father," calling his disciples into that same relationship. We are now able to see life through the eyes of Jesus, rather than focus on who Jesus is.

Science continues to unlock the secrets of the universe. James Lovelock speaks of the universe itself as Gaia, a living self-regulating organism of which we are the consciousness. Quantum sciences uncover non-material relationships among material objects that astound. Integral Theory deepens our understanding of politics, economics as well as philosophy. Advances in neurobiology continue to amaze us. It's magic all over again.

Once we are convinced of our deep connection with everything in the universe, we can begin to re-form our "Global Tribe" in ways that honor difference but include all, in order that all can thrive. Our expanded mind capacity, deep intuition and higher consciousness will recognize that planetary concerns rank above narrow group interests and we can look forward to an ordered world organized as a holistic, unified organism.

Transition: will occur when a new thinking system awakens!

The Three Faces of God

In his book *Integral Spirituality*, Ken Wilber shows how the world's understanding of Spirit can been viewed in a way that correlates with his quadrants. The face of God most familiar to the West is the second-person relationship between believers and a personal God. Like Martin Buber's dialogic I-Thou relationship, the interaction is mutual and intimate. The modern world is more comfortable relating to God, if at all, from a third person perspective, as an It. The marvels of creation, the beauties of nature move the soul to a deep sense of awe. The Eastern mind envisions an indivisible identification with the essence of the divine. This connection the great I-I is foreign to Western thought; but the mystics have always known and reveled in this relationship with the One Who Is. Each of these perspectives brings to the table important insights about the One Who Is Mystery.

We can see that Jesus related to God in all three ways.

[Third Person: The great I-It]   **The Greatness of God**

Jesus spoke: about God - he saw the infinite and glorious face of God in nature which is filled with the glory of God. He often reflected on the objective, natural face of God and used parables illustrating nature's connection with God and God's kingdom.

[Second-person: The great I-Thou]   **The Closeness of God**

Jesus spoke: to God - he saw the intimate and loving face of God as *abba*, the One he met in the quiet moments of prayer, the One who nurtured and guided him. Talking in intimate personal terms about God was as natural as breathing to Jesus.

[First person: The great I-I]   **The Godness of the Human Person**

Jesus spoke: as God - he realized that deep within him was the very image of the inner face of God. This presence of God was actually his own deepest, truest self, his supreme identity! He embraced his own inner divinity as he walked on the earth as God as well as with God.

For each person one or more of the faces may be difficult to imagine; but as our religious consciousness grows we will become more comfortable integrating the three. Each offers us a way to deepen our understanding of and relationship to the Great Mystery.

We are left then with three questions:

Is your God big enough??

God must be big enough to create, inhabit, and continue to evolve galaxies.

Is your God close enough?

God, the unfathomable God of the cosmos, comes to us like a close and caring parent.

Is your God you enough?

Jesus fully owned his Godself and invites us to do the same. He operated at the highest levels of consciousness manifesting his own divinity. His own eternal face was the face of God, the same divine face that is in every person.

Part VI

WDWGFH
[Where Do We Go From Here?]

The New Beginning
There's Always a Question

18

Ahead of Schedule

Society will reappear [not "reform."]

Stephen King. The Stand

As Turquoise gathers us together into a global community and calls us to find and/or recover the healthy stories, rituals, and the best heritage of all the "tribes" of the world. Adding these insights to the scientific, psychological, and sociological knowledge accumulated through time, WholeView consciousness will adopt a new myth large enough to hold and focus our complex relationships. This story will give meaning to a new way of living together.

Is Evolution the New Cosmic Myth?

Ken Wilber thinks so. "It's Evolution, Baby! Evolution is not done with us yet. On the contrary, it is still very much alive in humanity's tireless quest for greater meaning, greater purpose, and greater sophistication. It is this evolutionary impulse that keeps us moving forward, allowing modern science to emerge from magic and superstition, modern medicine from leeching and bloodletting, chemistry from alchemy, psychology from phrenology, astronomy from astrol-

ogy, democracy from theocracy, and the list goes on. Every field of human inquiry continues to move through wave upon wave of increasing accuracy, fidelity, and applicability. Integral is the next wave, and is already dramatically enhancing each of these fields—art, medicine, psychology, spirituality, sustainability, leadership, and many more—while also showing how they all fit together in a seamless totality of knowledge and understanding" (Ken Wilber: https://integrallife.com/video/brief-history-integral).

The God Connection

We have to figure out how to bridge our differences. Spirituality cannot be forced. People must discover it for themselves. What we believe is that culture must be shaped and kept spiritual. The spiritual rules must be maintained by those in charge. Otherwise, our people would be spoiled and lazy. Look at the indecency and degradation of your movies and music. And you hold your corrupt politics as something to be proud of?

I don't like parts of our culture, either. But freedom is important for men and women. What if the document is correct? You understand what it says. You've experienced the Alignment. What if people everywhere can learn to practice a spirituality that establishes the discipline you speak of, but is voluntary and engaged in because of the thrill of the experience? The Document is saying we can experience a Breakthrough of some kind. We have to figure out what that is. It could lead to a resolution between both sides. What if Armageddon doesn't have to happen?

James Redfield. The Twelfth Insight

Theologians and scientists alike are studying evolution for insights into the role it plays in our lives today. As Ken says, it's not over; but where is it manifest? Over millions of years, first matter and then living beings developed. We have seen how human consciousness continues to deepen and become capable of dealing with greater and greater complexity. The aspect that has remained unexplored is the spiritual realm. A man before his time, Jesuit scientist and scholar, Pierre Teilhard de Chardin saw God as the driving force of evolution.

Teilhard wrote in the 1930s but was censured by the church. His most famous works, published after his death in 1955; contributed to the rise of WholeView consciousness. Like Graves, Teilhard famous quote [from an essay included in his 1952 collection: *Toward the Future.*] situates humanity on the brink of a new endeavor. "The day will come when, after harnessing space, the winds, the tides, and gravitation, we shall harness for God the energies of love. And on that day, for the second time in the history of the world, we will have discovered fire."

The original Big Bang, now called the Flaring Forth by many evolutionists, can be seen as the explosion of God's love into the universe. God is evolving with the world; drawing it forward to greater and greater grandeur. Teilhard saw matter as spirit moving slowly enough to be seen. He held that humans are not material beings that have a spiritual experience; but spiritual beings having a human experience. Human consciousness enables humans to collaborate with God in creation.

Cynthia Bourgeault has written a book outlining the cosmic relationship within God, the Trinity that continues to expand outward through creation including all in its embrace. Cynthia sees this as the heart of Christianity, as Jesus was the first to fully comprehend its implications. Ilia Delio, a devotee of Teilhard, sees love not as the background of the human story; but as the human story itself. God is not a stay-at-home God, she says; God is a communion of Persons in love, eternally and dynamically in love. God is within us and ahead of us calling forth. God is the power of the future asking for our conscious participation as midwives of the new creation.

Does This totally Negate the Old Myth?

As long as it is taken where it lives, in the lower left quadrant at the Blue, TruthForce, level, the myths of the Book will always be needed. Children and adults whose consciousness are at the In-Doctrination and Parade stage faith levels rely on concrete stories for inspiration and direction. The religious imagination develops slowly and there will always be a place for all previous religious insight.

Does the Bible Have Anything to Say to Us Today?

Rereading anything from a more mature perspective always uncovers deep truths that were previously missed. This is especially true when it comes to religious literature. The words and stories hide precious insights lying in wait for the right moment to emerge. If you read the first and third chapter of Genesis carefully, you may notice that when the snake told Eve that if she ate the fruit she would be like God, he lied. According to the first chapter she already was the image of God! We didn't have to do anything to get there. We carry the Divine spark of creation within us. It has taken us until now to realize this much! And it's not over yet!

Where Do We Go From Here?

A lot needs to be done to repair the damage caused by the limitations of first tier consciousness. But as more and more people reach the Integral and WholeView stages the next problems will arise. What do we do now that we see these global connections? How can this web of relationships function effectively?

New worldviews will lead to new understandings of civilization as well as of Mystery:

The next colors and stages projected by Spiral Dynamics will be the:

- Coral ᵛMeme paralleling the Red and focusing on power followed by the
- Teal ᵛMeme paralleling Blue and focusing on order.

Epilogue:
Beyond Fantastick and Even More
Amazing

As Ender Wiggin's saga ends in Orson Scot Card's book *Children of the Mind*, three sentient species and a rogue yet fully conscious computer program interact in an attempt to survive. Jane, the computer program, was built thousands of years ago by the Hive Queens, an insect-like species who communicate telepathically, as a bridge to try to get the human Ender to realize that they were not a threat to humanity and did not need to be destroyed. [This is the plot of the original book and movie, *Ender's Game.*]

Now Starways Congress has been systematically shutting Jane down because "she" cannot be controlled. She has been offered refuge within the Fathertrees and the Mothertree of Lusitania. These trees are the third stage of life of the *pequeninos*, the third sentient life form on the planet. The Fathertrees cannot contain her and are afraid that the Mothertrees will be harmed by her presence. The Hive Queen assures Human, one of the Fathertrees that all will be well and she is right.

As Jane finds her way along the lace-like links among the trees, she finally finds the delicate web that was the Mothertree. It looked very delicate but did not break when she touched it. As she followed the web she found life, tiny lives hovering on the brink of consciousness. Underneath them lay a warm and loving aiúa [soul] that was in its own way strong though without ambition. The Mothertree was part of every life that dwelt upon her skin, yet was easy to break free from, for she expected nothing from her children. The Mothertree loved her children's independence as much as she had loved their need.

When Jane came to her, she looked upon Jane as she looked upon any lost child. She backed away and made room for her, let Jane taste of her life, let Jane share the mastery of chlorophyll and cellulose. There was room here for more than one. And Jane for her part, having been invited in, did not abuse the privilege. She did not stay long in any Mothertree, but visited and drank of life and shared the work of a Mothertree and then moved on, tree to tree, dancing her dance along the gossamer web. Now the Fathertrees did not recoil from her; for she was the messenger of the mothers, she had shared their life so she could be their voice. A thousand Mothertrees around the world, and the growing Mothertrees on distant planets, all of them found voice in Jane, and all of them rejoiced in the new, more vivid life that came to them because she was there.

When the others came into the forest they saw a strange dancing light that played up and down the trunk of the tree as Jane moved among them. But more amazingly there were blossoms on the tree. The trees had never blossomed before because the descolada virus had robbed them of that. As the *pequeninos* ate the fruit they sang the song of their rejoicing. And the Mothertree in the center of them was part of the song. Jane, the aiúa whose force and fire made the tree so much more alive than it had ever been before, danced into the tree, and along every path of the tree, a thousand times in every second.

It was a song of the season of bloom and feast. They had gone so long without a harvest that they had forgotten what harvest was. But now they knew what the descolada had stolen from them long before. What had been lost was found again. And those who had been hungry without knowing the name of their hunger were fed.

> Orson Scott Card. *Children of the Mind.* New York: Tom
> Doherty Associates 1996, pp. 200 – 207.

Fantasy or Fantastik?

Boy meets girl; becomes species meets species. Good science fiction, like good religion, always pushes the boundaries. In 1960, when the Fantastiks opened the world seemed simple; but the play hinted that all was not as it seemed. In 2015, the world seems on the brink of chaos and destruction; but perhaps this too is an overly simplistic evaluation. There are those, there will always be those, who hold up a light. Those willing to open their minds and hearts to rescue planets and civilizations. They stand as small communities living out their belief that we are all connected. And when they are attacked, they hold out their hands and say, with the small community in Starhawk's *The Fifth Sacred Thing*, there is always room for you at the table. Prayer at this deepest level offers its energy to the Love that is the universe with the hope that, like the pictures on the cave walls, we will attract the spirits once again.

May our hunger be filled and our thirst assuaged.
¡Que nunca tengas hambre! ¡Que nunca tengas sed!

Starhawk. *The Fifth Sacred Thing*

Books That Contribute
to the Conversation

Armstrong, Karen. *The Case for God.* New York: Alfred Knopf, 2009.

Bourgeault, Cynthia. *The Holy Trinity and the Law of Three: Discovering the Radical Truth at the Heart of Christianity.* Boston: Shambala Press, 2013.

Carse, James. *The Religious Case against Belief.* New York: Penguin Books, 2008.

Delio, Ilia. *The Emergent Christ: Exploring the Meaning of Catholic in an Evolutionary Universe.* Maryknoll, NY: Orbis Books, 2014.

_____. *The Unbearable Wholeness of Being: God, Evolution, and the Power of Love.* Maryknoll, NY: Orbis Books, 2013.

Delio, Ilia. ed. *From Teilhard to Omega: Co-creating and Unfinished Universe.* Maryknoll, NY: Orbis Books, 2014.

Fasching, Darrell and Dell Dechant. *Comparative Religious Ethics: A Narrative Approach.* Malden, Massachusetts: Blackwell Publishing, 2001.

Fox, Matthew. One *River, Many Wells.* New York: Jeremy Thatcher/ Putnam, 2000.

Gafni, Marc. *Your Unique Self: The Radical Path to Personal Enlightenment.* Tucson, AZ: Integral Publishers, 2012.

Greeley, Andrew. *The Catholic imagination.* Berkley: University of California Press, 2000.

_____. *The New Agenda: A Proposal for a New Approach to Fundamental Religious Issues in Contemporary Terms.* New York: Image Books, 1975.

Haidt, Jonathan. *The Righteous Mind.* New York: Pantheon Books, 2012.

Haught, John. *Deeper than Darwin: The Prospect for Religion in the Age of Evolution.* Cambridge, MA: Westfield Press, 2003.

Johnson, Elizabeth. *Ask the Beasts: Darwin and the God of Love.* London: Bloomsbury Publishing Plc, 2014.

_____. *Quest for the Living God: Mapping Frontiers in the Theology of God.* New York: Continuum International Publishing Group Inc., 2008.

Jones, Tom and Harvey Schmidt. *The Fantasticks: The Complete Illustrated*

Text. New York: Applause Theatre Book Publications, 1990.

Keen, Sam. *Hymns to an Unknown God*. New York: Bantam Books, 1994.

_____. *The Passionate Life: Stages of Loving*. San Francisco: Harper, 1992.

LeShan, Lawrence. *The Psychology of War: Comprehending Its Mystique and Its Madness*. New York: Helios Press, 2002.

Lovelock, James. *Gaia: A New Look at Life on Earth*. London: Oxford University Press, 1979

_____. *The Vanishing Face of Gaia: A Final Warning*. New York: Basic books, 2010.

McIntosh, Steve *Evolution's Purpose: An Integral Interpretation of the Scientific Story of Our Origins*. New York: SelectBooks, Inc., 2012

_____. *The Presence of the Infinite*: *The Spiritual Experience of Beauty, Truth, Goodness*. Wheaton, IL: Quest Books, 2015.

O'Murchu, Diarmuid. *God in the Midst of Change: Wisdom for Confusing Times*. Maryknoll, NY: Orbis Press, 2012.

_____. *In the Beginning was the Spirit: Science, Religion and Indigenous Spirituality*. Maryknoll, NY: Orbis Books, 2012.

Polkinghorne, John. *Quarks, Chaos, and Christianity: Questions to Science and Religion*. New York: Crossroads, 1997.

_____. *Science and Religion in Quest of Truth*. New Haven, CT: Yale University Press, 2011.

Rumi. *Hidden Music*. translated by Azima Kolin & Maryam Mali. London: Thorsons, 2001.

_____. *The Soul of Rumi*. Translated by Coleman Barks. San Francisco: HarperSanFrancisco, 2001.

Sanguin, Bruce. *Darwin, Divinity and the Dance of the Cosmos: An Ecological Christianity*. BC, Canada: CopperHouse Books, 2007.

_____. *The Emerging Church: A Model for Change and a Map for Renewal*. Kelowna, BC, Canada: CopperHouse Books, 2008.

Smith, Paul. *Integral Christianity*. St. Paul, MN: Paragon House, 2011.

Smith, Wilfred. *The Meaning and End of Religion*. Minneapolis, MN: Fortress Press, 1991.

Spong, John Shelby. *Eternal Life: A New Vision Beyond Religion, Beyond Theism, Beyond Heaven and Hell*. New York: Harper Collins, 2010.

_____. *Jesus for the Non-Religious: Recovering the Divine at the Heart of the Human*. New York: HarperOne, 2007.

Teilhard de Chardin, Pierre. *The Divine Milieu*. New York: Harper & Row, 1965.

_____. *Hymn of the Universe*. New York: Harper & Row, 1961.

Wilber, Ken. *Integral Meditation: Mindfulness as a Path to Grow Up, Wake Up and Show Up in Your Life*. Boulder, CO: Shambhala, 2016.

_____. *Integral Spirituality: A Startling New Role for Religion in the Modern and Postmodern World*. Boston: Integral Books, 2006.

_____. *A Sociable God: Toward a New Understanding of Religion*. Boston: Shambhala Publications, 2005.

Integral Studies Resources

Articles:

Clare Graves: "Human Nature Prepares for a Momentous Leap"
http://www.clarewgraves.com/articles_content/1974_Futurist/1974_Futurist.html

Don Beck: Stages of Social Development   http://www.integralworld.net/beck2.html   **Steve McIntosh:** Premises and Principles of an Evolutionary Worldview http://www.culturalevolution.org/docs/ICE-Philosophy.pdf

Sites:

Great Intro to Spiral Dynamics - http://www.transpersonalscience.org/vidspiral1.aspx

Don Beck: Spiral Dynamics Integral - http://www.spiraldynamics.net

Chris Cowan: Spiral Dynamics - http://www.spiraldynamics.orgGraves/colors.htm

Ken Wilber: Integral Institute - http://www.integralinstitute.org/

Bruce Sanguin: Blog for Evolving Mystics - http://brucesanguin.com/

Paul Smith: Integral Christianity - http://www.broadwaychurch-kc.org/

Steve McIntosh: Integral Consciousness - http://www.stevemcintosh.com/

Thoughts from Other Worlds

Bradley, Marian Zimmer. *Darkover Series*
Cameron, James. *Avatar*
Card, Orson Scott. *The Ender Series*
Collins, Suzanne. *The Hunger Games*
Donaldson, Stephen. *The Chronicles of Thomas Covenant*
Herbert, Frank. *The Dune Series*
King, Stephen, *The Stand*
Lem, Stanislaw. *Solaris*
Levin, Ira. *This Perfect Day*
Lewis, C.S. *The Chronicles of Narnia*
_____. *Space Trilogy*
Rand, Ayn. *Atlas Shrugged*
_____. *The Fountainhead*
Redfield, James. *The Celestine Prophecy*

Roth, Veronica. *Divergent Series*
Quinn, Daniel. *Ishmael*
Starhawk. *City of Refuge*
_____. *The Fifth Sacred Thing*
Tolkein, J.R.R. *The Hobbit, The Lord of the Rings*
Wachowski, Andy. *The Matrix Trilogy*

Index

Made in the USA
Middletown, DE
12 September 2020